THE THEBAN LEGION
286
NEARLY 6,000 BATTLE-HARDENED TROOPS WERE EXECUTED AFTER REFUSING TO FOLLOW THE EMPEROR'S ORDER TO KILL ALL THE CHRISTIANS IN BURGUNDY.

BARTHOLOMEW
CA. 70
FLAYED AND THEN CRUCIFIED IN MODERN-DAY ARMENIA IN A PLOT HATCHED BY PAGAN RELIGIOUS LEADERS.

PETRUS RAMUS
1572
KILLED BY A PARIS MOB ALONG WITH THOUSANDS OF OTHER PROTESTANTS, HIS BODY WAS MUTILATED, DECAPITATED AND THROWN INTO THE SEINE RIVER.

CHESTER A. "CHET" BITTERMAN III
1981
TAKEN HOSTAGE AND KILLED BY COLOMBIAN GUERILLAS. BEFORE GOING TO COLOMBIA, HE WROTE, "I FIND THE RECURRING THOUGHT THAT PERHAPS GOD WILL CALL ME TO BE MARTYRED FOR HIM IN HIS SERVICE IN COLOMBIA. I AM WILLING."

MARION HARVIE
1681
"I DIE NOT AS A FOOL OR EVIL-DOER, OR AS A BUSYBODY IN OTHER MEN'S MATTERS; NO, IT IS FOR ADHERING TO JESUS CHRIST, AND OWNING HIM TO BE HEAD OF HIS CHURCH."

DONALD CARGILL
1681
"THE LORD KNOWS I GO UP THIS LADDER [TO BE EXECUTED] WITH LESS FEAR AND ANXIETY THAN I EVER ENTERED THE PULPIT TO PREACH. FAREWELL ALL RELATIONS AND FRIENDS IN CHRIST; FAREWELL ALL EARTHLY ENJOYMENTS, WANDERINGS AND SUFFERINGS. WELCOME JOY UNSPEAKABLE AND FULL OF GLORY."

PAUL CARLSON
1964
MISSIONARY DOCTOR SHOT BY SIMBA REBELS IN THE CONGO.

THOMAS CRANMER
1556
RECANTED HIS FAITH UNDER TORTURE, THEN REPENTED AND BOLDLY PROCLAIMED HIS FAITH BEFORE THE FIRE. HE LOWERED HIS RIGHT HAND—WHICH HAD SIGNED HIS RECANTATION— INTO THE FLAMES FIRST.

EZZAT HABIB
2005
RUN OVER BY A TAXI TO SILENCE HIM FROM PREACHING THE GOSPEL TO MUSLIMS IN EGYPT.

CYPRIAN
258
AFTER KNEELING IN PRAYER, HE GAVE HIS EXECUTIONER A GIFT, THEN PLACED THE BLINDFOLD ON HIMSELF, SURRENDERING HIS LIFE PEACEFULLY AND TREASURING THE LIFE TO COME.

ALBAN
304
THE FIRST MARTYR IN BRITAIN; THE SECOND WAS THE EXECUTIONER ORDERED TO KILL HIM WHO, AFTER HEARING ALBAN'S TESTIMONY, BECAME A CHRISTIAN ON THE SPOT AND REFUSED TO FOLLOW THE ORDER.

JOHN FRITH
1533
BURNED AT THE STAKE ON JULY 4, 1533.

POLYCARP OF SMYRNA
CA. 155
DISCIPLED BY THE APOSTLE JOHN, HE WAS STABBED BY THE ROMANS AFTER THE FIRE SET TO BURN HIM WOULD NOT TOUCH HIM. "EIGHTY-SIX YEARS I HAVE SERVED HIM, AND HE HAS DONE ME NO WRONG. HOW CAN I BLASPHEME MY KING WHO SAVED ME?"

JEROME OF PRAGUE
1416
HUNG BY HIS HEELS FOR 11 DAYS AND LATER BURNED AT THE STAKE, HIS LAST WORDS WERE, "THIS SOUL IN FLAMES I OFFER CHRIST TO THEE."

IGNATIUS OF ANTIOCH
107
MARTYRED AT THE COLISEUM IN ROME: "NOW I BEGIN TO BE A DISCIPLE. COME FIRE AND CROSS AND GRAPPLINGS WITH WILD BEASTS, THE RENDING OF MY BONES AND BODY...ONLY LET IT BE MINE TO ATTAIN JESUS CHRIST."

LIU HAITONG
2000
DIED FROM BEATINGS AND NEGLECT IN A CHINESE PRISON AFTER BEING ARRESTED FOR ATTENDING AN UNREGISTERED CHURCH MEETING.

THEOPHANE VENARD
1861
BEHEADED IN WHAT IS NOW VIETNAM.

JOHN ROGERS
1555
"THAT WHICH I HAVE PREACHED I WILL SEAL WITH MY BLOOD."

BONNIE WITHERALL
2002
GUNNED DOWN IN LEBANON, WHERE SHE WORKED IN A CLINIC AS AN AVENUE TO SHARE THE GOSPEL.

JIM ELLIOT, PETE FLEMING, ED MCCULLY, NATE SAINT, ROGER YOUDERIAN
1956
MISSIONARIES TO ECUADOR; THEIR DEATHS SERVED TO CALL A GENERATION TO MISSIONS.

JOHN KLINE
1864
"GOD DOES NOT ACQUIESCE IN THE INJUSTICE AND WRONG THAT IS BEING PERPETRATED IN THE WORLD."

YONA KANAMUZEYI
1964
PROVIDED SANCTUARY TO FLEEING HUTUS IN RWANDA'S GENOCIDE. CAPTURED BY SOLDIERS AND EXECUTED AFTER PRAYING FOR THEM.

MAURICE TORNAY
1946
"DEATH IS THE HAPPIEST DAY OF OUR LIVES. WE MUST REJOICE IN IT MORE THAN ANYTHING, BECAUSE IT IS OUR ARRIVAL IN OUR TRUE HOMELAND."

MANCHE MASSEMOLA
1928
BEATEN TO DEATH BY HER OWN MOTHER AFTER ATTENDING PRE-BAPTISM CLASSES WITH HER COUSIN.

EDMUND CAMPION
1581
"IF OUR RELIGION DO MAKE TRAITORS, WE ARE WORTHY TO BE CONDEMNED; BUT OTHERWISE WE WERE AND HAVE BEEN TRUE SUBJECTS AS EVER THE QUEEN HAD."

NAMUGONGO MARTYRS
1886
FORTY-FIVE MEN, CATHOLICS AND PROTESTANTS, AGES 12 TO MID-50S, WERE ROLLED TIGHTLY IN COMBUSTIBLE LEAVES, AND THEN PLACED IN FIRE NEAR KAMPALA, UGANDA.

THE FORTY MARTYRS OF SEBASTE
320
FORCED TO STAND, NAKED, ON A FROZEN LAKE BECAUSE THEY REFUSED TO RENOUNCE CHRIST.

WATCHMAN NEE
1972
DIED AFTER A LONG IMPRISONMENT IN COMMUNIST CHINA.

ROBERT SOUTHWELL
1595
PUT ON THE RACK 13 TIMES IN THE TOWER OF LONDON, THEN HUNG.

JOHN MAZZUCCONI
1855
MARTYRED BY NATIVES HE HAD COME TO MINISTER TO ON A SOUTH PACIFIC ISLAND.

REDOY ROY
2003
TIED TO HIS BED AND STABBED TO DEATH IN BANGLADESH FOR SHOWING THE JESUS FILM.

ALPHAGE
1012
THE DANES COMMANDED A RANSOM OF GOLD TO RELEASE ALPHAGE, THE ARCHBISHOP OF CANTERBURY. "THE GOLD I GIVE YOU IS THE WORD OF GOD," HE REPLIED BEFORE BEING BLUDGEONED TO DEATH BY HIS CAPTORS.

JOHN
CA. 98
TORTURED AND EXILED TO PATMOS.

JOHN COLERIDGE PATTESON
1871
CLUBBED TO DEATH ON THE ISLAND OF NUKAPU. "I AM QUITE AWARE THAT WE MAY BE EXPOSED TO CONSIDERABLE RISK . . . BUT I DON'T THINK THERE IS MUCH CAUSE FOR FEAR."

BERNARD MIZEKI
1896
SPEARED TO DEATH IN WHAT IS NOW ZIMBABWE.

CHRYSOSTOMOS
1922
"IT IS DURING THE HIGH SEAS THAT THE GOOD SAILOR STANDS OUT, AND IT IS DURING TIME OF TRIBULATIONS THAT THE GOOD CHRISTIAN DOES THE SAME."

REV. JOSE JUAN LOZADA CORTEZA
2003
SUSPECTED FARC GUERRILLAS PULLED HIM OFF A BUS AND EXECUTED HIM BESIDE THE ROAD.

WALTER MILL
1558
"A HUNDRED SHALL RISE OUT OF MY ASHES, WHO SHALL SCATTER YOU, YE HYPOCRITES AND PERSECUTORS OF GOD'S PEOPLE."

GEORGE BLAUROCK
1529
BEFORE BEING BURNED AT THE STAKE HE WROTE IN A HYMN: "THY SPIRIT SHIELD AND TEACH ME, THAT IN AFFLICTIONS GREAT, THY COMFORT I MAY EVER PROVE, AND VALIANTLY MAY OBTAIN, THE VICTORY IN THIS FIGHT."

JAMES THE LESS
63
STONED TO DEATH IN SYRIA.

GEORGE AND ELLEN GORDON
1861
CLUBBED TO DEATH IN ERROMANGA AFTER FOUR YEARS OF TEACHING THE BIBLE AND CARING FOR THE SICK.

A NIGERIAN WOMAN
2006
POLICE DID NOT EVEN GET HER NAME BEFORE THE MUSLIM MOB BEAT HER TO DEATH FOR SHARING CHRIST WITH MUSLIMS.

PHILIP
54
CRUCIFIED AND STONED.

WILLIAM TYNDALE
1536
BURNED AT THE STAKE FOR TRANSLATING THE BIBLE INTO THE ENGLISH LANGUAGE.

WILLIAM SWINDERBY
1401
DIED AT THE STAKE IN LONDON.

PATRICK HAMILTON
1527
BURNED AT THE STAKE; THE FIRE WAS SET LOW SO THAT HE SUFFERED FOR SIX HOURS.

HENRY FOREST
1529
SMOTHERED IN A CELLAR JAIL.

PETER
69
CRUCIFIED UPSIDE DOWN BY THE ROMANS.

FELIX MANZ
1527
PLACED ON A BOAT, TAKEN OUT ON RIVER LAMMAT NEAR LAKE ZURICH, BOUND, WEIGHTED AND THROWN INTO THE WATER. "I PRAISE THEE, O LORD CHRIST IN HEAVEN, THAT THOU DOST TURN AWAY MY SORROW AND SADNESS...ALREADY BEFORE MY END HAS COME, THAT I SHOULD HAVE ETERNAL JOY IN HIM."

FRANCISCO MONTOYA
2004
SHOT IN THE HEAD FOR MINISTERING WITHOUT PERMISSION IN AN AREA CONTROLLED BY FARC GUERRILLAS IN COLOMBIA.

JOHN SMITH
1824
SENTENCED TO DIE BY A BRITISH MILITARY COURT FOR TEACHING SLAVES IN GUYANA TO READ.

PASTOR MARIANO DÍAZ MÉNDEZ AND PASTOR JAIRO SOLÍS LÓPEZ
2003
KILLED FOR THEIR MINISTRY WORK IN CHIAPAS, MEXICO.

MAXIMILIAN KOLBE
1941
CATHOLIC PRIEST WHO VOLUNTEERED TO DIE IN PLACE OF ANOTHER PRISONER AT AUSCHWITZ.

DIETRICH BONHOEFFER
1945
HANGED BY ORDER OF ADOLF HITLER. "THIS IS THE END—FOR ME, THE BEGINNING OF LIFE."

COLLIN LEE
2005
HIS MINISTRY IN SUDAN BROUGHT HIM INTO THE GUNSIGHT OF THE LORD'S RESISTANCE ARMY.

HENRY LYMAN
1834
SPEARED AND EATEN BY BATAK WARRIORS ON THE ISLAND OF SUMATRA, INDONESIA.

At Any Cost

THE FAITHFUL WITNESS OF OUR PERSECUTED CHRISTIAN FAMILY

VOMBOOKS
The Voice of the Martyrs

TABLE OF CONTENTS

At Any Cost

VOM Books
A division of The Voice of the Martyrs
1815 SE Bison Rd.
Bartlesville, OK 74006

ISBN 978-0-88264-209-3

Printed in South Korea

202112p014b2

INTRODUCTION

Let us journey together with our persecuted brothers and sisters to the ends of the earth!

Praise God that through faith in Christ, we are His sons and daughters. God's great family includes our Christian brothers and sisters throughout all time and from around the world. What a wonderful blessing it is for us to be included in such a family — for all eternity!

At VOM, we serve persecuted Christians in the most difficult and dangerous places for God's people to live — hostile areas and restricted nations where those who serve Christ suffer violence, imprisonment and even death for their faith and witness. Despite the risk and suffering, God's great family is working to bring Him glory and advance His kingdom in *every* nation on earth.

On His way to the cross, Christ prayed that all who believe in Him would become one, completely united in Him and in God's service. When we take Christ's prayer seriously and enter into fellowship with our persecuted Christian family members, we strengthen His body and advance His kingdom in four important ways: God is glorified; persecuted Christians are encouraged; we are inspired by their example of bold and sacrificial faith; and our love for other members of the body of Christ serves as a powerful witness to the lost world.

God has promised that "the earth will be filled with the knowledge of the glory of the LORD as the waters cover the sea" (Habakkuk 2:14), and He showed the Apostle John "a great multitude that no one could number, from every nation, from all tribes and peoples and languages, standing before the throne and before the Lamb" (Revelation 7:9). These prophecies and promises are being fulfilled in our time. Let us joyfully commit, through prayer and willing hearts, to pay any price in God's service.

We pray that this book will be a useful companion in your journey of fellowship with our persecuted brothers and sisters. As you pray through its pages during personal prayer time or with your family, group or class, you will be inspired by the faith and faithfulness of Christian family members who boldly follow Christ at the ends of the earth — places few of us have seen and about which many of us have never even heard.

PRAY FOR THE PERSECUTED

Remember those who are in prison, as though in prison with them, and those who are mistreated, since you also are in the body.

—Hebrews 13:3

HOSTILE

This includes nations or large areas of nations where national governments attempt to provide protection for the Christian population, but Christians are routinely persecuted by family, community members and/or extremist groups because of their witness.

RESTRICTED

This includes countries where government-sanctioned circumstances or anti-Christian laws lead to Christians being harassed, imprisoned, killed or deprived of possessions or liberties because of their witness. Also included are countries where government policy or practice prevents Christians from obtaining Bibles or other Christian literature. In addition to government persecution, Christians may also experience persecution from family, community members and/or extremist groups.

*Learn how to pray for our persecuted Christian family in each country through our Global Prayer Guide at **vom.org/prayerguide.***

AFRICA

Our persecuted Christian brothers and sisters in Africa face a myriad of daily challenges, including political instability, seemingly nonexistent borders, tribal conflicts and attacks from Islamist groups like Boko Haram and al-Shabab. In addition, Muslims are becoming radicalized at an alarming rate, and neighboring Middle Eastern countries are pouring resources and funding into Islamic missionary activities that seek to convert Christians to Islam by force or allurement. Despite these difficulties, our persecuted Christian family members are obediently sharing the gospel. And many Muslims, disillusioned by the lies and violence of Islam, are turning to faith in Christ.

The suffering endured by Christians in Niger has drawn many to Christ. "Persecution became fertilizer for the gospel," a front-line worker said. In parts of Niger that have suffered strong persecution, evangelists have observed a greater eagerness among new believers to apply biblical principles to their lives.

In some areas of Africa, entire villages and tribal groups are leaving Islam to follow Christ. For example, the Yao tribal group in southeastern Malawi, northwestern Mozambique and southern Tanzania has experienced a remarkable move of the Holy Spirit. In what some consider one of the greatest gospel movements in all of Africa, a tribe that traditionally believed to be Yao is to be Muslim has turned to Christ in great numbers.

Along with these advances of God's kingdom among Muslims across Africa, Christians there continue to witness boldly for Christ despite the risks. Nigerian widows show forgiveness to those who murdered their husbands and even share the love of God with them. In Ethiopia, when religious extremists destroy homes and churches to silence any witness for Christ, our persecuted brothers and sisters respond with unwavering faith amid their suffering. In Uganda, believers who are rejected by their families and driven from their homes because of their faith offer forgiveness to family members and seek ways to bear witness for Christ. And Somali believers are sharing the gospel despite the real threat of death if discovered.

Across the African continent, enemies of the gospel try to silence any witness for Christ. Yet God's kingdom continues its advance as our persecuted Christian family members remain faithful to Him and obedient to His Great Commission.

One generation
shall commend your
works to another,
and shall declare
your mighty acts.

—Psalm 145:4

Enemies of the gospel try to hinder the advancement of God's kingdom in Africa by indoctrinating children with false teachings, such as those found in Islam. Preparing the next generation in countries like Sudan (*p. 6*), the Central African Republic (*right*) and Nigeria (*facing page*) is essential in helping our youngest brothers and sisters stand courageously for Christ among those trying to silence their Christian witness.

Christians in many parts of Africa faithfully witness for Christ in regions ravaged by violence and war, such as conflict areas in Sudan. Islamists have bombed villages and churches, displacing hundreds of thousands of people in their efforts to Islamize African nations and eradicate Christians from the region. Shell casings and abandoned tanks become an everyday sight for those who live there.

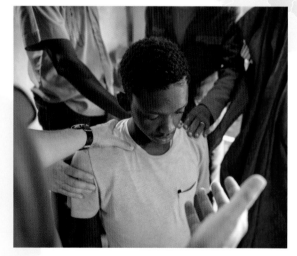

VOM provides training and support to churches as our Christian brothers and sisters take great risks to minister in Jesus' name. And when their villages and homes are destroyed, displaced Christians receive assistance, such as food and other necessities, through front-line workers who become the "hands and feet" of Jesus.

At one outreach event in Sudan (*left*), local pastors traveled to surrounding villages to minister and share the gospel. Within a few days, so many wanted to hear the Good News that some had to stand outside and listen through church windows. In one day, 300 people placed their faith in Christ, and 70 of them were former Muslims.

THANKING GOD IN THE FLAMES

FAIZAH AND NAGAWO

Faizah and her husband, Nagawo, were raised as Muslims, but after coming to faith in Christ they began reaching out to Muslims with the gospel and helping new believers mature in faith. For three decades, they served the church in Ethiopia and helped former Muslims who suffered persecution after leaving Islam. Then they became targets of persecution themselves.

One night while Faizah was home with her daughter and granddaughter awaiting Nagawo's return, several nearby houses went up in flames. As the Islamists responsible for igniting the fires approached her house, Faizah called out to God, "Lord, if my soul is Yours, deliver us from this!"

The men dragged Faizah and her family outside, then set the house ablaze. "Lord, if this fire is from You," Faizah prayed, "let it continue. No one can stop it. But if this fire is from the devil, let it be extinguished."

Shortly after she prayed, a sudden rain extinguished the fire. Faizah was grateful, but then she heard a frightening shout from a celebrating Islamist: "We killed the main person! The leader is dead!"

Faizah's heart sank. She followed the crowd until her worst fears were confirmed and she saw Nagawo's lifeless body lying on the ground. She wept in horror and waited by his body until help arrived the next morning.

Later, Faizah learned that the Islamists had killed Nagawo because he, a former Muslim, had led many others to leave Islam and place their faith in Christ. Though her loss was great, her faith remained firm.

"Even while the flames were shooting up, I was thanking God," she said. "And even when I saw that my husband had died, I maintained my relationship with Jesus. For the past 30 years, I have been intimately serving Jesus. He has helped me to pass through these difficulties, and I believe that He will help me even more."

Following Nagawo's death and the loss of her home, Faizah and her family struggled to support themselves, living under a plastic tarp on her church's land for more than a year. She eventually got connected with VOM, who helped rebuild her home and continues to provide other forms of support.

Even after all she has lost, Faizah bears no grudge against Nagawo's killers, and she wants to continue reaching Muslims with the gospel.

"Even though I lost my husband," she explained, "when I saw [the Muslims'] lives and how they live, I know that I'm living in the right way. I want them to come to Christ."

Christians in Africa are targeted not only by governments, terrorist groups and religious extremists but also by family members, a painful reality that many of our brothers and sisters know too well. Yet their faithful witness endures, advancing God's kingdom no matter the cost.

"And a person's enemies will be those of his own household. ... Whoever finds his life will lose it, and whoever loses his life for my sake will find it."

—Matthew 10:36, 39

Front-line workers in countries like Sierra Leone (*left*) joyfully baptize new believers in nearby streams. At one gathering, front-line workers baptized 36 new Christians to the accompaniment of villagers singing "I Have Decided to Follow Jesus." Christians sometimes also receive a print or audio Bible.

"Each time I open my Bible during my studies, it reminds me of God's faithfulness. Seeing the ashes of some pages I could no longer read makes God's Word more alive in my heart. This is what I am still holding onto."

—Rebekah, from Nigeria, after finding her Bible in the rubble following a Boko Haram attack in which her family was killed and her home destroyed

While Christians in some countries, like Sudan (*left*) and the Central African Republic (*right*), can attend church openly, it is not without risk. But other African countries are far more restricted; in some, it is illegal to convert to Christianity, access to Bibles is extremely limited and churches must meet in secret.

> "Even though [Muslims] were hating me and they are still trying to kill me, something in my inner being said, 'Love.' My portion is just to love them and reach out to these people."
>
> —Jemal, an Ethiopian Christian whose Muslim family sent a mob after him

Ugandan Christians (*right*) face severe persecution in the Muslim-majority border regions as neighboring Arab countries pour resources into advancing Muslim interests in the country. Churches in Uganda respond to the growing influence of radical Islam by reaching out to their neighbors in love, training their leaders to share the gospel with Muslims and caring for former Muslims who are persecuted for leaving Islam to follow Christ.

MINISTRY IN THE NUBA MOUNTAINS

MORRIS AND CABINA

Pastor Morris and his wife, Cabina, have no indoor plumbing, electricity or cellular service, and the region where they live has been bombed repeatedly. But they still find ways to serve God right where He has put them.

Morris pastors a church in the Nuba Mountains, a majority-Christian region that the Sudanese government has bombed heavily in efforts to expel Christians and Islamize the country. In addition to his church responsibilities, Morris coordinates VOM help for Christians in the area, distributing Bibles and Christian materials; receiving medicines for distant clinics; and organizing blankets, clothing and food for displaced believers.

He and Cabina host an average of at least two dozen people in their simple home every day. Cabina not only cooks and cleans for their daily house guests but also helps many orphans who have lost their parents in the conflict. She enlists the help of women in her community to feed and make clothing for them. "Many orphans are naked," she said. "[There is no one to] care for them." She also teaches the women to make baskets, mattresses and floor mats for their own families.

While Cabina helps meet the needs of guests, orphans and local women, Morris visits Muslim prisoners of war being held in his village. Many have asked him why he visits them, since some served the government that bombed his village. "Because Jesus says we have to love our enemies," Morris replies. "Even if they are killing us, we have to love them."

Cabina sometimes worries about Morris as he coordinates relief and visits Muslim prisoners of war. "When I think about what could happen," she said, "I become worried about my husband." But she knows he is carrying out Jesus' command to share the gospel with everyone — even enemies — and she trusts His promise to be with us to the ends of the earth. "Then my worry goes away and I know that God is in control," she said.

Morris and Cabina know that life is easier and safer in other parts of the world, but they are committed to serving God where He placed them. During a trip to a country that was not at war, Morris was asked by a fellow traveler why he intended to return to war-torn Sudan. "How can I stay in a comfortable place while my people are dying?" he replied. "I will go back to my people."

Living and ministering in a place where many have been killed in bombings is a special calling, and Morris and Cabina embrace it together. "To be a Christian doesn't mean just to have a good and easy life," Morris said. "It means maybe you live in the hard times. We as Christians can do it by the power of God and by the grace of God."

> "Whatever is happening today will pass tomorrow. What strengthened us in these events will become our story. We have faith that one day Christ will avenge us."
>
> —Pastor Timothy, Nigeria

Whether it's providing food to displaced Christians in the Central African Republic (*facing page*) or Ethiopia (*left*), or distributing Bibles to indigenous people groups in Africa (*above*), VOM is ready to meet the needs of our persecuted Christian family members and ensure that every Christian in a hostile area or restricted nation has a Bible.

In Kenya (*below*), agriculture provides a unique opportunity to share the gospel with those who might otherwise never hear it. Amina, a former Muslim, grew up as a member of the nomadic Borana tribe, who measure their wealth in cattle. After she came to faith in Christ, she gave audio Bibles in the Borana language to others in her tribe. "They can put in their earphones and listen while they are herding animals," she said. "The audio Bibles have changed them."

It takes great courage and faith to openly worship and serve Christ in northeastern Nigeria, where nearly all Christians have lost family members in attacks by Boko Haram and Fulani Islamic militants. Access to food and education are often limited by ongoing violence, and thousands of Christians live in camps for internally displaced people.

SUDAN

ERITREA

DJIBOUTI

ETHIOPIA

SOMALIA

UGANDA

KENYA

TANZANIA

COMOROS

Front-line workers in Africa travel to rural villages and churches to encourage and disciple Christians wherever they are. They know their lives are at risk every time they venture out, as radical Muslims have ambushed travelers along the road with impunity. Yet these bold witnesses choose to take the gospel to these areas despite the risk. "I prefer going to places where people are struggling or they don't know Jesus," one pastor said.

TUNISIA

MOROCCO

ALGERIA

LIBYA

MAURITANIA

MALI

NIGERIA

CENTRAL AFRICAN REPUBLIC

BURKINA FASO   CAMEROON

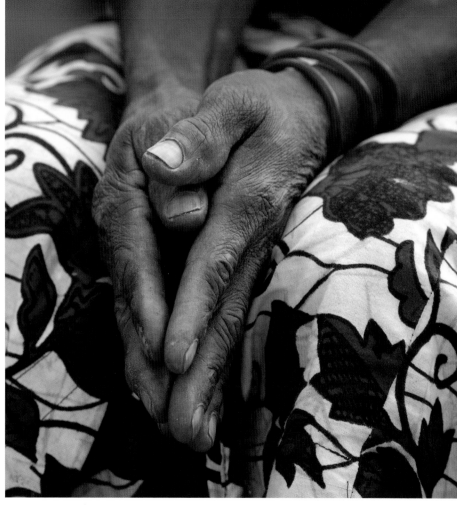

Our Nigerian brothers and sisters offer radical forgiveness to their persecutors, advancing God's kingdom through their faithful witness. When Fulani farmers in one village asked a Christian widow to pray for rain, she asked them why they wanted her to pray. After all, some of them had been responsible for her husband's death. "Your God is more powerful than ours," they replied.

"The larger body of Christ cares about me? Wow. I'm extremely glad, incredibly happy. I just find joy being a part of the family of Christians."

—Ibrahim, Nigeria

When our persecuted Christian family members receive help and prayer support from the global body of Christ, they know they are not alone or forgotten. Whether in the Central African Republic (*facing page*) or Nigeria (*left*), the joy of fellowship with the global body of Christ is evident on their faces.

While Uganda is a majority-Christian nation with many active churches, local Islamists persecute Christians in some regions, and Christian converts from Islam are especially targeted. Still, churches in Uganda continue to reach out to their neighbors and train leaders how to share the gospel with Muslims.

FORGIVING HER HUSBAND'S KILLERS

ALICE

Alice and her family were asleep when men with covered faces stormed into their home and called for her husband by name. When he opened the bedroom door, they shot him.

As her husband lay dying on the floor, Alice tried to stop the bleeding while their five children cried in terror. Nigerian soldiers arrived at their village about an hour later and took him to the hospital, but it was too late. Alice's husband died on the way to surgery.

In Nigeria, attacks like these are common. Thousands of Christian women have been widowed in raids on Christian villages by Boko Haram terrorists and Fulani Islamic militants. These women are often completely disregarded after losing their husband. In Nigerian culture, married women are the responsibility of their husband and his family, so they receive little to no support from their own family.

That was Alice's situation after her husband's death. She struggled to provide for her children as a single parent, staying in their family home and continuing to farm their plot of land. Then, a year and a half later, Fulani Islamic militants struck again, burning Alice's entire village.

Alice and her children fled on foot, taking shelter in a nearby village. They moved from house to house, living in tight spaces with Christian families who offered them a place to stay, be it a hallway or a studio apartment. Alice was overwhelmed by raising her children and starting over on her own, but she resolved not to give up. "I am not dead yet," she thought, so she asked God to give her wisdom.

Alice eventually met some VOM workers who helped her relocate and rent a simple home. After so much suffering, she was ready for a fresh start. But before she could settle into her new home, she faced yet another crisis. Fulani Islamic militants attacked her village and others in the area, killing dozens and injuring many more. Alice and her family, along with several other VOM-supported widows, were displaced by the violence, and VOM workers again helped Alice's family relocate.

Despite all that Alice has experienced at the hands of Fulani Islamic militants, she still doesn't resent them or desire revenge. When she saw a neighbor whom she recognized as her husband's killer, she summoned the courage to approach him and greet him kindly. She tries to do the same with any Fulani person she meets. "I have never felt anger toward them," she said, "because the Bible already said that this would happen and said we should watch and pray."

Although she has experienced one trial after another, Alice sees how God has carried her through each tragedy. "The Word encourages me all the time, because it says the Lord gives and the Lord takes," she said. "We are just here for a time. Right now, I am no more afraid; I am not afraid because of my God."

> "I have never felt anger toward them."
>
> —Alice, speaking of her husband's killers

Thousands of women have lost their husbands in violent attacks by Fulani Islamic militants and Boko Haram, who target Christians throughout northern Nigeria in an attempt to silence their witness for Christ. But amid their suffering, these widows have found God's grace to be sufficient, empowering them to forgive their enemies and reach out to them with the love of Christ.

Whether meeting for a cup of freshly roasted and brewed coffee (*left*) or gathering for worship in a church (*above*), Christians in restricted nations and hostile areas are strengthened through fellowship with their brothers and sisters in Christ.

This young pastor (*left*) goes from house to house and farm to farm sharing the gospel with ethnic Somalis in Kenya. While some respond with interest, others become hostile; Somalis who leave Islam to follow Christ often face severe persecution from family and community members. But God's kingdom is advancing as bold evangelists faithfully witness for Christ despite opposition.

Living in community with other believers is a blessing for our persecuted brothers and sisters. It is something they long for and desperately seek, especially after being rejected by family members for leaving the religion of their family and culture.

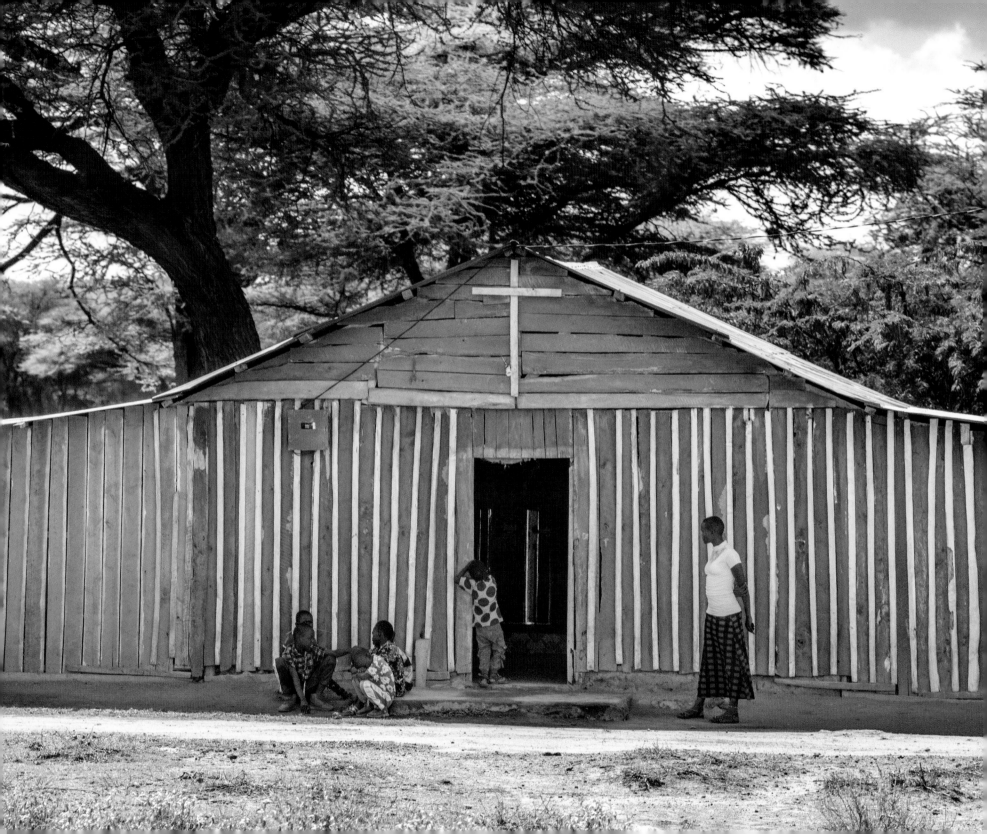

Even as radical Islam grows at an alarming rate across Africa, entire communities are being transformed by believers' commitment to share the Good News. Our persecuted brothers and sisters testify to the truth of the gospel by reaching out to their neighbors with the love of Christ, forgiving their persecutors and displaying joy amid suffering.

From the Sahara Desert in the north to the Swahili Coast in the east, our Christian family members eagerly proclaim the gospel throughout Africa amid persecution from governments, terrorist groups, religious extremists and their own family members. May their testimonies of faithfulness and joy inspire us to a deeper commitment to Christ and His Great Commission.

LATIN AMERICA

Some of our Christian brothers and sisters in Latin America live with the daily reality of atheistic communism, while others face syncretistic Christo-pagan oppression. Yet even amid these obstacles, bold believers maintain their witness for Christ with joy and perseverance.

In Cuba, churches face unrelenting pressure from a government committed to communism's atheistic ideology. The Cuban government seeks to control all aspects of religious life, banning the construction of new church buildings, forbidding believers from meeting in unregistered churches and pressuring Christian leaders through recurring interrogations and arrests. The authorities' actions, however, have served only to unite church leaders in Cuba across denominational lines, encouraging them to join in fellowship and in proclaiming the gospel.

In southern Mexico, Christians face continual threat of violence from drug cartels, Marxist guerrillas and groups that blend pagan rituals with religion. Some local authorities and entire communities actively persecute Christians, driving them from their homes and villages because of their faith in Christ.

Yet a renewed church-planting effort has arisen amid this opposition, as our brothers and sisters in southern Mexico joyfully continue to advance God's kingdom in their suffering. Front-line workers Paty and Jaime labored for years sharing the gospel among the unreached indigenous Mixteco people in southern Mexico. And when Jaime was suddenly killed because of his ministry work, Paty resolved to continue the work even in her immense grief. "My way to honor the memory of my husband is to follow the work he was doing," she said.

God is also working through the bold faith of believers in Colombia's "red zones," where Christians suffer extreme violence at the hands of Marxist guerrillas and paramilitary groups. Some former guerrilla fighters have become front-line workers after coming to faith in Christ, preaching the gospel with great courage in areas where they once fought for atheistic ideals. One such worker is Rolo, who delivers Bibles in some of Colombia's most dangerous areas. As a former guerrilla, Rolo has unique access to those who live and work in red zones. "Give me the Bibles and the gasoline to take them, and I'll get them there," he says.

While worship and evangelism are risky in some parts of Latin America, our brothers and sisters continue to bear witness for Christ in some of the most dangerous places for Christians on earth.

In remote parts of southern Mexico, following Christ comes at great cost. Christians often lose their homes, jobs, inheritances and land because of their faithful witness. Providing them with backpacks containing Bibles and other basic necessities shows them that the body of Christ cares about them and that they are not forgotten.

Left: This church is located in one of Colombia's "red zones," areas controlled by violent Marxist guerrillas and paramilitary groups. These groups often force churches to close, locking their doors and threatening anyone involved in worship or corporate prayer. Despite the risks, our Colombian brothers and sisters in Christ find ways to gather for worship, prioritizing obedience to Christ over all.

TAKING THE GOSPEL INTO THE JUNGLE

DAVID AND GLORIA

When David and Gloria met while attending missionary school, they both felt called to share the gospel in the jungles of Colombia. Since their marriage, they have lived and ministered for nearly two decades in a guerrilla-controlled "red zone" known for drug trafficking and violence. They work faithfully to plant churches, train church leaders, distribute Bibles and build relationships among the region's various people groups.

In their work to advance God's kingdom, they have experienced threats and opposition from all sides as the government, paramilitaries, rebel groups and organized crime syndicates have vied for control of territory. They have even been driven from communities by local religious groups, but they have persisted, knowing that their work is worth the risk. "We had to decide if we were going to leave or stay," David said. "Our decision was to stay because we were preaching the gospel."

The spiritual development of children is an important part of David and Gloria's approach to reaching Colombians for Christ. Guerrilla groups often lure children into their ranks, and thousands of Colombian children are raised in guerrilla camps and trained as fighters from a young age. So to encourage them to follow Christ instead of the rebel groups, David and Gloria teach the Bible to hundreds of children weekly, picking them up in their villages with a boat provided by VOM.

While raising children in an area plagued with violence and unrest comes with a risk, David and Gloria intentionally involve their three children in their ministry work as part of their spiritual education. And they are thankful for the opportunity to inspire other families to engage in ministry. "It has been a privilege to preach the gospel and to be a testimony to many other families," David said. "Sometimes people say they don't go to the field because they have kids, but we tell them, 'You can! You can do ministry; you can work and your kids will be fine.'"

Working among armed rebels is stressful, though, and David and Gloria's children have expressed fear and anxiety when traveling through guerrilla territory. But they overcome their fear through unwavering faith and encouragement from other believers. "I am not afraid," their daughter, Samantha, said, "because I know that God is protecting us and there are a lot of people praying for us when we do this."

Knowing that their Christian brothers and sisters are praying for them gives the entire family the strength and encouragement to continue sharing the love of Christ in Colombia's red zones. "Thank you for going with us to these places," Gloria said. "Through your prayers, we go together. We don't do this alone."

Facing page: Ministering as a family can be challenging, but David and Gloria confidently encourage others to involve their children in ministry work. Although their children have experienced situations that caused fear and anxiety, they have also seen how God provides and takes care of them.

Communist rebels and paramilitary groups, funded by drug trafficking, brutally oppress those in Colombia's lawless "red zones" who have no means of defending themselves. These violent groups routinely abuse children, bomb churches and murder anyone who opposes them. Yet our Christian family members in Colombia bear witness to God's truth despite the obstacles. May their faithfulness inspire us to a greater obedience to Christ and His Great Commission.

> "For whoever does the will of God, he is my brother and sister and mother."
>
> —Mark 3:35

After a group of Christians were expelled from their village in southern Mexico, they took refuge in homes provided by a local church and a VOM-supported front-line worker. Those families were then able to open a small grocery store, giving them the opportunity to share the gospel in their new community.

Distributing Bibles in Colombia is physically demanding, both because of the quickness with which workers must distribute the Bibles to avoid being noticed by one of the armed groups and because of the primitive or non-existent roads. What may normally be a six-hour motorcycle ride can extend to two days during the rainy season. Still, bold believers accept the risk of taking Bibles to pastors and churches in remote areas where access to God's Word is limited.

CUBA

SOUTHERN
MEXICO

COLOMBIA

God is working through the bold faith of believers in Cuba, southern Mexico and Colombia, where our brothers and sisters continue to bear witness to Christ in some of the most dangerous places for Christians on earth. Their faithful obedience is costly, as many in this region have given their lives for the sake of the gospel. Yet God's kingdom continues to grow despite those who try to hinder the gospel's advance.

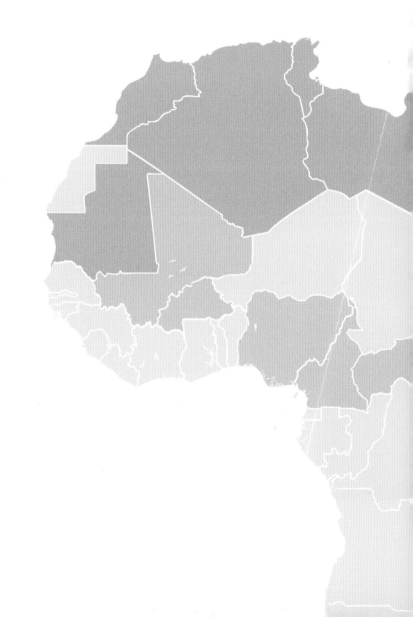

The children of pastors and front-line workers are not exempt from risk. One family's 9-year-old son was struck by stray bullets from guerrilla gunfire while out running errands with his mother. And guerrillas threatened to kidnap the teenage daughter of another family if they didn't stop their ministry work. Still, our youngest brothers and sisters happily join their parents in advancing the gospel. "I really like being in the ministry," said the teenage daughter of one pastor. And her 7-year-old brother expressed a similar passion for the Lord's work. "When I play with kids in the village," he said, "they see Jesus in me."

Left: Before Liliana was born, her parents moved to one of Colombia's most dangerous areas to serve as church planters. Tragically, when Liliana was 13, Marxist guerrillas killed her father because of his ministry work. Though her faith wavered after her father's murder, Liliana stands firmly on the spiritual foundation he helped build and is now training to be a missionary.

"My desire is to take the gospel to the difficult areas where nobody else wants to go. That's where God has called me. That is where my heart is."

—Andres, a Colombian pastor
who ministers in the "red zones"

Facing page: Rivers are the main transportation arteries in some parts of Colombia, and boats are an essential tool not only for moving supplies but also for visiting church members and bringing people to church. Front-line workers must be creative when delivering Bibles and ministry supplies in these areas. They face the constant risk of confrontation with violent groups that may be lurking along the riverbank.

Right: Isolated communities in southern Mexico have little access to God's Word, and Bibles in the region's indigenous languages are especially rare. Since those living in remote villages are often unreceptive to Christian workers from outside the area, front-line workers sometimes start by telling Bible stories. Then, when someone wants to know more about a story, the front-line worker offers him or her a Bible.

My soul longs for your salvation; I hope in your word.

—Psalm 119:81

NO PERMISSION REQUIRED

OUR BROTHERS AND SISTERS IN CUBA

In the last years of Fidel Castro's life, Cuba's strict communistic and atheistic ideals appeared to be eroding. Then, around 2014, the waning spirit of the Communist revolution revived, and pressure on Christians rose sharply. Since then, our Cuban brothers and sisters in Christ have faced more subtle forms of persecution as the government has attempted to silence their Christian witness.

But as the communist spirit has continued to grow, so has the passion of Christians in Cuba to reach their countrymen with the gospel. Amid the oppressive environment of Cuba's Communist government, Christian leaders from various denominations rallied to launch an evangelistic campaign in Havana. The strategy was simple: Believers would go to bars, cafes and parks to share the gospel.

When Communist officials heard about the campaign, they summoned church leaders from all denominations for interrogation. But since the evangelistic effort was not tied to a central leader or organization, Cuban authorities had no one to arrest and no way to stop it. Our brothers and sisters in Christ, therefore, continued to share their faith boldly throughout Havana.

After one of the believers shared about Jesus in a public park, a man asked him who had given him the authority to evangelize there. "I didn't ask Raul Castro for permission to talk about Jesus," the believer replied boldly, "and I'm not going to ask you for it, either."

Throughout Cuba, our brothers and sisters in Christ continue to courageously worship and proclaim the gospel amid governmental oppression and hostility, demonstrating that God's love is far greater than the spirit of Cuba's Communist revolution.

These Christians (*above*) are praying during a celebration at which more than 100 new believers received baptism. "In the middle of threats, the church in Cuba continues," said a front-line worker who ministers in the country.

As more people in Cuba come to know Christ, the need for Bibles continues to grow. There are no Christian bookstores in Cuba, and the government allows the sale of Bibles only to members of the ecumenical Protestant church organization. Even when a Bible is available, it can cost a third of a worker's monthly income. Over the years, believers have used a variety of methods to bring Bibles into Cuba, including by boat, by hand-carrying individual copies and through government-approved shipments. Sometimes a clandestine printer can also produce Bibles.

As our persecuted Christian family members suffer for their faith, they exemplify the words of the Apostle Peter: "But rejoice insofar as you share Christ's sufferings, that you may also rejoice and be glad when his glory is revealed" (1 Peter 4:13). They exude a deep, abiding joy as they faithfully follow Christ at any cost.

"Give me the Bibles and the gasoline to take them, and I'll get them there."

—Rolo

Above and right: For years, Rolo has delivered Bibles to remote communities throughout Colombia. He has unique access to some of the most dangerous areas because he was once a member of a guerrilla rebel group.

"God said His Word doesn't return void; it has to keep advancing," said Sara, a former guerrilla who is now a front-line worker in Colombia. Because of Sara's ministry work distributing Bibles and reaching guerrillas with the gospel, she and her family have been targeted by a violent rebel group and forced into hiding. Still, they continue their work because they know God has called them to share His Word and lead others to faith in Him. "If you aren't doing anything for God," Sara said, "you aren't doing anything."

ADVANCING THE GOSPEL AT ANY COST

PATY AND JAIME

When Paty and Jaime decided to become missionaries, their hearts were set on serving in Turkey. But over time, they each felt led to work among unreached, indigenous people groups in their home country of Mexico. Shifting their focus from Turkey to the nearly 500 Mixteco communities in Guerrero state, they prayed and searched for a place to serve.

While the Mixteco share ancestry, their communities are diverse, speaking nearly 50 distinct languages and sometimes harboring animosities toward one another and outsiders. Paty and Jaime reached out to three different communities before one finally agreed to let them live in their village.

Even that community, however, was not quick to welcome them. On several occasions, villagers openly told them they were unwelcome and that they would be cut to pieces if they stayed. But Paty and Jaime pressed on faithfully, working hard to cultivate trust with their neighbors over the next two years.

In an intentional effort to become valued community members, Jaime joined the other men in grueling physical labor and Paty spent hours with the women baking at the communal oven. "We tried to give the people dignity, to be the incarnational presence of Christ," Paty said. "Jesus came in humility, so that's what we tried to do."

Seeing Paty and Jaime's efforts to fit in, some of the villagers softened toward them. And eventually a few people asked what religion they followed. Knowing they could quickly close doors to the gospel if they talked about Christ directly, they chose instead to share Bible stories. They encouraged villagers with biblical examples in response to life's concerns, and when villagers wanted to know more, they gave them Mixteco audio Bibles.

The couple slowly gained the trust and respect of many community members. So when anyone tried to stir up trouble against them, the town elders and others came to their defense. Still, some remained hostile to Paty and Jaime's presence.

One day, after Jaime failed to show up for a meeting with Paty and their mission leaders, Paty received the heartbreaking news that her husband had been killed. While the circumstances of his death are uncertain, it was clearly not an accident; his body showed evidence of trauma.

Jaime's death left an enormous void in Paty's life. But amid her grief, she resolved to continue the kingdom work that she and Jaime had begun. "My way to honor the memory of my husband is to follow the work he was doing," she said.

Paty and Jaime's faithfulness bears witness to the cost of advancing the gospel in hostile areas and restricted nations — an obedience to proclaim Christ at any cost.

Our persecuted Christian family members place high importance on reaching children with the gospel. In Colombia, a front-line worker has developed an after-school music program to keep children off the streets and out of the coca fields. He uses music to teach the children that they are valued by a God who loves them, and some of his former students now lead worship in local churches. Another front-line worker, in southern Mexico, operates an after-school program in which children receive a free meal and learn Bible stories and songs. In Cuba, Christian teachers work to counteract the communist indoctrination children receive in school by sharing the truth of the gospel.

I will cause
your name to be
remembered in all
generations; therefore
nations will praise
you forever and ever.

—Psalm 45:17

Right: Illustrated children's Bibles are an effective means of sharing God's Word with both adults and children in many parts of Latin America. For adults who don't read well or are intimidated by traditional Bibles, the colorful, engaging illustrations of biblical stories help them learn Scripture as they grow in faith. "It draws them in," a Colombian front-line worker said.

Jaime gave his life working to advance the gospel in southern Mexico (see p. 29). His favorite verse was Habakkuk 2:14, "For the earth will be filled with the knowledge of the glory of the LORD as the waters cover the sea." Jaime dreamed of planting a church in his community and painting that verse on the side of the church. May his faithful witness and that of countless other Christians in Latin America inspire us to share Christ in our communities with that same boldness.

Dear heavenly Father, we stand beside our Christian brothers and sisters who serve in some of the most dangerous parts of Latin America. We thank You for their faithfulness in working to advance Your kingdom. We pray that their faith will grow daily as they are nourished by Your Word. Renew their souls through Your Spirit, and give their leaders wisdom and direction. Amen.

THE MIDDLE EAST AND CENTRAL ASIA

God's kingdom continues to advance across the Middle East and Central Asia, where Christians living under Islamic oppression face increasing opposition.

In the Middle East, the global body of Christ is witnessing the greatest movement of Muslims turning to Christ since the foundation of Islam. Stories of Muslims professing faith in Christ after experiencing dreams and visions of Him have become commonplace, and faithful believers obediently share the gospel with their Muslim friends and families despite the risk.

In Iran, where the government restricts access to Bibles and Christian literature, evangelism is thriving and discipleship is a high priority. Although many Iranian Christians have been arrested, interrogated and imprisoned, they remain faithful to Christ.

Across the Arabian Peninsula, a number of Saudis and Yemenis also have placed their faith in Christ. But with the increase in conversions has come an increase in persecution. Still, believers carefully witness for Christ, knowing the risk.

In Iraq and Syria, civil war and attacks by Islamists have driven thousands of Christians from the region, leaving a small but bold and faithful remnant. As Muslims there become increasingly disillusioned by the rampant corruption and violence among radical Islamic groups, Christians are provided a unique opportunity to share the gospel with those desperate for hope and truth.

Across Central Asia, which includes the former Soviet republics of Azerbaijan, Kazakhstan, Kyrgyzstan, Tajikistan and Turkmenistan, Christianity remains restricted in various ways. Christians in Central Asia are persecuted by authoritarian governments as well as the Muslim majority.

While all churches in this region are required to register, the government routinely denies them registration. Therefore, most believers meet in unregistered churches, where they are subject to fines and even jail time if discovered. In some countries, like Tajikistan, children under age 18 are forbidden from attending even registered churches.

In the Central Asian nation of Pakistan, the challenges of following Christ are compounded by poverty, corruption and radical Islam. Christians are often bound to lives of poverty by jobs that amount to little more than indentured servitude. And they live under the constant threat of being falsely accused of blasphemy against Islam, the Quran or Muhammad. Nevertheless, bold Pakistani believers continue to witness to their Muslim neighbors, baptize new Christians and work tirelessly to equip and encourage their brothers and sisters in Christ. And in Afghanistan, Christians face continued opposition from Islamic extremist groups like the Taliban and by family members.

As governments and Islamists seek to silence their Christian witness, believers are working to advance God's kingdom across the Middle East and Central Asia. May their example encourage and inspire us to do likewise!

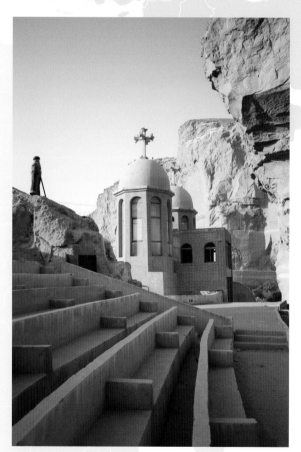

Our brothers and sisters in Egypt share the gospel throughout North Africa and the Middle East. The Christian leader pictured above has been targeted by Islamists because of his ministry work, but he willingly risks his life to reach Muslims for Christ and remains steadfast in his commitment to the Great Commission. "Jesus has given me this ministry," he said. "He gives me the courage. He gives me the peace to do it. He gives me the capability to do it. When He gives us a ministry in our life, we are responsible for what it costs us."

The path to Christ for an Egyptian convert is not a smooth one. When Nour came to faith in Christ, her fanatical Muslim husband abused her and threw her out of the home, leaving her and their children homeless. Nour eventually remarried. When her father reported them to the police, they fled to another city, where their children were cursed and harassed in school. After local Islamists labeled them infidels deserving death, they were forced to flee again.

"I want to be part of the church even if it costs me. I love this suffering life for [Christ]."

—Dilek, a Christian from Sudan who fled to Egypt to escape hostile family members and the oppressive Sudanese government

From the grasslands of the Kazakh Steppe in Kazakhstan to the Karakum and Kyzylkum deserts in Turkmenistan and Uzbekistan, the landscape of Central Asia is as varied as the region's people groups and languages. Pray that the gospel will spread throughout Central Asia and that "the glory of the LORD shall be revealed, and all flesh shall see it together, for the mouth of the LORD has spoken" (Isaiah 40:5).

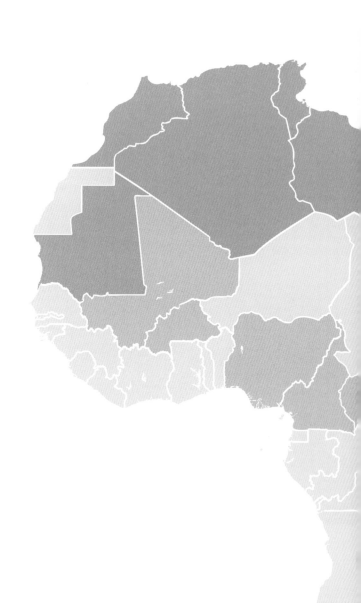

Introducing the gospel while meeting a person's physical needs is a powerful way of sharing the love of Christ in restricted nations. In one restricted Middle Eastern nation, front-line workers approached a young boy selling socks in the marketplace, and the boy gratefully accepted their gift of a memory card loaded with Christian materials.

Caught in the crossfire between warring Muslim factions, Syrian Christians as well as Muslims have suffered greatly during the civil war. Hundreds of thousands of Syrians were driven from their homes and now live in refugee camps in neighboring countries *(above and facing page)*. Amid the conflict, however, Muslims are turning to Christ in significant numbers as believers reach out with acts of compassion, demonstrating the hope and love of Christ.

Stories of Muslims coming to faith in Christ after having a dream or vision are common throughout the Muslim world. Many Christian converts from Islam describe having seen a man in white in their dream, an experience that becomes a turning point in their path to faith. The dreams serve as one element leading to a saving knowledge of Christ.

THE COST OF FAITH AND FORGIVENESS

KHALED AND SAMIRA

On the morning of Sept. 11, 2001, Khaled led the call to prayer at his mosque in Yemen. Already wrestling with doubts about his Muslim faith, he watched in horror as Muslims celebrated the terrorist attacks on the United States. The attacks and reaction to them in the Muslim world persuaded him to leave Islam immediately.

Khaled was still struggling with his beliefs when he encountered a stunning example of God's grace in a socialist newspaper. There, he read the words of Christ from John 8:7 — "Let him who is without sin among you be the first to throw a stone at her." Those words shattered everything Khaled had believed about Christians.

As he continued his search for truth, Khaled learned about a new Christian radio program in a Yemeni dialect. As he began listening to the program in secret, he was awed by Christ's teaching on forgiveness and love. Khaled contacted the program's hosts to learn more about the Christian faith, and after weeks of discussions he placed his faith in Jesus Christ.

Khaled secretly obtained a Bible and continued to learn and grow as a believer. Soon, he began attending regular Bible study in a nearby city, and his frequent trips alarmed his wife, Samira. When she eventually confronted him about the trips, he admitted that he was a Christian.

Khaled eagerly told Samira that Jesus had changed his life and that He could change hers, too. Samira had noticed the changes in Khaled, and after learning the cause she also placed her faith in Christ. For two years, the couple kept their faith secret, until deciding to make a public profession through baptism.

After the family's home address and photos of Samira's baptism were obtained and circulated by radical Muslims, Khaled and Samira suffered harassment and beatings from former friends and colleagues.

Then, Samira's nephew attacked her in public, beating her, breaking her arm and dragging her down the street. Khaled tried to file a police report, but the police said she deserved the beating because she was a Christian.

Khaled and Samira made plans to flee Yemen. But those plans were tragically altered one morning when Khaled was awakened by his son shouting, "Father! Mother is on fire in the kitchen!" Someone had apparently snuck into their home and replaced Samira's jar of cooking oil with gasoline.

Khaled and his son frantically tried to put out the fire, suffering burns in the process, and Samira was taken to the hospital with third-degree burns covering the upper half of her body. When the hospital staff learned that she was a Christian, they began treating her poorly, and Samira died after receiving an injection of a questionable substance from her doctor.

Soon after Samira's death, Khaled and his children left Yemen. Adjusting to a new country hasn't been easy, but Khaled has expressed forgiveness for those who persecuted his family and caused his wife's death.

And Khaled has seen God working through his family's suffering. "When I think about our story," he said, "the only thing I can think is that God is preparing us for something bigger … to serve Him. It is in layer after layer of persecution that He changes us to be like Him."

Nearly all Yemenis are Muslims, and converting to Christianity from Islam is a crime punishable by death. Families consider it extremely shameful for a family member to become a Christian. Amid this reality, the gospel has flourished. Steady numbers of Yemenis are being added to the body of Christ as believers reach out in creative ways that are both bold and wise.

The Iranian government is among the most oppressive in the world. Christians in Iran face constant threat of criminal charges and imprisonment for owning Bibles or even talking about Christ. Yet amid this oppression, the bold and faithful witness of our Christian brothers and sisters has drawn hundreds of thousands of Muslims to the hope found only in Jesus Christ.

"Be still, and know that I am God. I will be exalted among the nations, I will be exalted in the earth!"

—Psalm 46:10

Muslims throughout the Middle East and Central Asia seek salvation through the fulfillment of religious duties, hoping their works will save them. A former Muslim from another part of the world explained this truth well, saying, "I had never heard of salvation before in Islam. There's nothing like that. Your salvation is only by your good deeds. Even then, Allah will decide whether you go to paradise or not. There is no assurance." After trusting their salvation to the work of Christ, new converts from Islam willingly risk their lives for baptism to express publicly the joy and peace they have found in Him.

Left: Although the gospel spread throughout Turkey in the first century, fewer than 1% of Turks are Christians today, and most Turks consider Islam to be part of their national identity. Despite opposition from their family members, communities and all levels of government, bold believers work to advance God's kingdom, strategically sharing the gospel in busy marketplaces or over a cup of coffee.

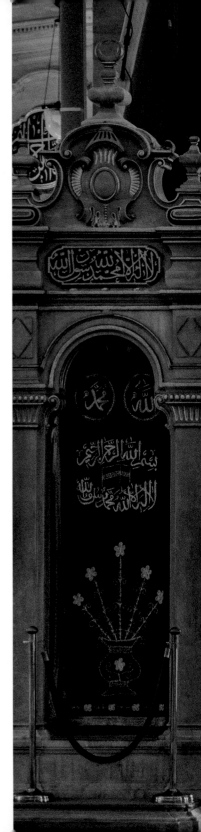

Our brothers and sisters in the Middle East are often targeted by radical Muslims when they leave Islam to follow Christ. Amir, a Christian in the Middle East, received an ominous phone message while traveling: Stop your son from attending church or "reap what you sow with your only son." The message was from an Islamic extremist group that knew Amir and his family had become Christians. The Islamist also asked Amir what kind of financial support he received from the church. Amir boldly replied, "The only support they are giving me is the joy and peace of having Jesus Christ as my Savior."

Facing page: Since Rebekha Bibi became a believer in 2003, she has been persecuted by her Muslim family and by community members in Pakistan. She ministers door to door in an area that includes both Hindus and Muslims.

A BOLD WITNESS AMONG WOLVES

FADI

As Fadi was driving home after finishing his ministry work one hot July day, four Islamic extremists began shooting at his car, causing him to lose control and flip the vehicle down a steep hillside. While he lay unconscious in the wreckage, the attackers scrambled down to his car, tore up his Bibles, stole his gospel tracts and left him for dead.

The attack was the first of many that Fadi would encounter while ministering to Syrian refugees along the Lebanon-Syria border. But he continues to work in this dangerous region because he believes the gospel is too valuable not to share — even in areas controlled by Islamists. Fadi distributes food and shares the gospel with Muslims through relationship-building and storytelling. He also leads more than 30 house churches on both sides of the border.

The risk is great not only for Fadi but also for the former Muslims he disciples. A few of the young men he has led to Christ have been kidnapped by Islamists and held for ransom. And others have been brutally murdered because of their faith in Christ.

After Fadi shared his testimony with a group of Syrian Muslims one day, showing the scars from his bullet wounds and explaining that he still loved and wanted to serve the Syrians who had shot him, a young man named Mehri responded in faith. Mehri accepted Christ immediately, telling Fadi that Jesus had been visiting him in his dreams, and three months later he publicly professed his faith through baptism. But one month after Mehri's baptism, a group of fanatical Lebanese and Syrian Muslims broke into his house and slit his throat in front of his family.

When Fadi told Mehri's story to a local police official, in hope that he would investigate the murder, the two soon became friends. The police official now shares security concerns with Fadi and warns him of areas to avoid, but Fadi still chooses to share Christ with those living in dangerous areas.

In addition to sharing the gospel with Muslims, Fadi serves with other Christian workers at an education center for Syrian refugees. Many children of Syrian refugees have been out of school for several years, and the education center provides them with both educational and spiritual instruction. The Christian workers read to the children from *The Action Bible* each day, sharing the love of Christ while providing for their physical needs.

Despite the risks, Fadi continues his relentless ministry work in a region where he knows it is dangerous to share the gospel. He asks for prayer as he shares the love of Christ with lost Syrians. "We are all commandos for Jesus, to promote His love and forgiveness," he said. "Please pray for us."

Because Lebanon has a significant Christian population and its government protects the freedom of worship, the country has become a safe haven for displaced Christians throughout the region. Many evangelical churches in Lebanon have welcomed and cared for Syrian refugees, whether Christian or Muslim. These Muslim refugee children attend a school run by believers who love them.

In Muslim-dominated Central Asia, Christians go to great lengths to get God's Word into the hands and hearts of children so they can continue to grow in faith. Christian workers realize these young believers are the future of the church in Central Asia.

Receiving a care package like an Action Pack filled with basic necessities and a Bible brings joy and hope to persecuted Christians in places like Pakistan (*right*), where Christians are treated as second-class citizens. Anila, a young Pakistani Christian who lives at home with her father who abuses alcohol, was greatly encouraged when VOM provided her with a new backpack filled with essentials and a copy of God's Word. "After receiving the backpack," a front-line worker said, "she now believes that one day her father will be changed by the grace of God, and the joy of their family will be restored."

Workers distribute aid (*below*) and children play (*right*) at a Syrian refugee camp in Lebanon's Bekaa Valley. Syrian Christian converts living in these camps understand well the spiritual truth that this world is not our home.

Therefore let us go to him outside the camp and bear the reproach he endured. For here we have no lasting city, but we seek the city that is to come.

—Hebrews 13:13–14

Although Islam is the dominant religion in the Middle East, many have grown disillusioned with the violent extremism resulting from some of its teachings. And as Muslims have been forced to flee the violence in their homelands, believers in more open countries have taken the opportunity to share the gospel with them.

"Dying for Jesus would be a privilege for me. I have counted the risk and deemed it worth it for the sake of the gospel."

—Timur, a former Muslim who shares the gospel in Central Asia

The collapse of the Soviet Union caused economic hardship for many in Central Asia. Churches, however, have recognized the need to meet people's physical as well as spiritual needs, and they do so knowing the risk. When Olga came for a meal at a church's homeless ministry, she struggled with alcoholism and lacked the support of her husband, who was in prison. Today, the two of them are following Christ, and Olga serves as the cook for the homeless ministry.

ADVANCING THE GOSPEL IN IRAN

SHAHROKH

Shahrokh was struggling with drug addiction when he came to faith in Christ. So after overcoming the addiction, he began leading an addiction-recovery group that provides a way for him to share the gospel in a country where it is illegal to leave Islam. Drug addiction is a significant problem in Iran, and Christians like Shahrokh have found that working with recovery groups is a good way to share their eternal hope in Christ while helping others overcome addiction.

The work is risky, though. Anyone caught leading a Muslim to Christ can be charged with "acting against national security," a common charge against Christians in Iran. So when Shahrokh was summoned to meet with Iranian security officials about his work, he had a good idea of what to expect. The security officials tried to corner him with questions during the interrogation, but Shahrokh responded with wisdom and boldness, which had a powerful effect on the officials.

With the number of Muslims turning to Christ growing rapidly, the officials asked Shahrokh to help them understand who was leading so many Iranians to abandon Islam to follow Jesus. Shahrokh's answer left them in awe.

"You cannot stop the work of God," he replied. "You cannot block the divine methods God uses to meet human beings. You can close Christian social activities and house groups or put Christian workers in prison, but you cannot stop people seeing dreams or visions. You cannot put Jesus in prison. You cannot stop the work of the Holy Spirit."

The security officials dismissed Shahrokh, and he has not heard from them since. While he knows he could be interrogated again at any time, he continues to help Iranian Muslims free themselves from drug addiction and find true freedom in Christ.

Right: Because of Pakistan's blasphemy laws, Christians are at constant risk of being falsely accused of blaspheming Islam, the Quran or Muhammad. Still, sharing about Christ is legal under Pakistani law, and several bold evangelists take advantage of the opportunity to share the gospel publicly. Some front-line workers have been abducted and held for several days for sharing the gospel openly, while others have been beaten or slapped. They are willing to suffer harassment in order to share Christ with those who don't know Him.

After front-line workers placed Bibles and Christian literature in the back seat of a taxi in Iran, the driver distributed them to the believers in his secret house church. When the driver called to express his gratitude for the Bibles, his wife also got on the phone and said, "Can I really have my own Bible?" She had never owned a personal copy of God's Word, as it is illegal in Iran to own, print, import or distribute Bibles. "I always prayed that I would have my own Bible," she said. Kamran and Soro (*bottom left*) served in Iran for more than 10 years before they were both arrested. They have since fled to a nearby country, where they continue to disciple Iranian Christians remotely.

Left: Iraqi believers have a unique opportunity to share the gospel with those seeking hope and truth. Violence and instability under the country's oppressive Islamic government have caused many Muslims to become more open to the gospel. Despite threats from Islamists, Iraqi Christians are bearing witness to the truth of the gospel.

The people who walked in darkness have seen a great light; those who dwelt in a land of deep darkness, on them has light shone.

—Isaiah 9:2

A CHAIN OF DISCIPLESHIP

BALUAN, SHOKAN AND TEMIR

Standing on the street of a large Central Asian city, three men tease each other while hailing a taxi. Their deep and obvious affection for one another mirrors the bonds of faith and brotherhood they share — bonds formed by God's grace, as each of them left Islam to follow Christ.

Their journeys of faith and friendship began when Baluan, who grew up hating Christians, reached a crossroads as he searched for truth. Though deeply devoted to Islam, his sisters were Christians, and they faithfully shared the gospel with him over many years. Eventually, Baluan cried out to God to reveal whether Christianity or Islam was the true way. The next morning, he awoke convinced: "I understood that Jesus was for me Lord and Savior."

Baluan immediately began telling others about the hope he now had in Christ.

Shokan, a contractor Baluan had hired to build his kitchen, could not figure out why his client wanted to pray in the name of God the Father. As a Muslim, his understanding of God differed from Baluan's, and the two-day job for which he was hired stretched into two months as the men fell into lengthy discussions about life and religion.

At the end of two months, Shokan committed his life to Christ. And that same day, as a crowd of about 100 Muslims was leaving the mosque near his house, Shokan boldly proclaimed the gospel to them.

"Jesus … died for your sin," he told them. "If you go to the mosque, you cannot get saved."

As Shokan's enthusiasm for evangelism grew, he began inviting members of his community to his home to watch soccer matches. While they were there to watch the matches, he shared the gospel with them. He eventually led his wife and younger brother to faith in Christ. Then, with Baluan's encouragement, he moved to a nearby village where there were no Christians and planted a church.

Meanwhile, Baluan continued sharing the gospel in his village. His witness eventually led a coworker named Temir to begin asking questions about God. Then, two years to the day from when Shokan had accepted Christ, Temir also became a believer.

Baluan, Shokan and Temir have all matured in faith as Baluan has discipled the two newer believers, who in turn are now discipling others. The three brothers in Christ continue to add new links to their chain of discipleship as they proclaim the Good News in Central Asia.

"After a while," said a front-line worker who spent time in jail for her faith, "the fear just goes away and a boldness comes."

Above: Christian media, such as magazines, television and radio programs, are effective ways of getting God's Word into nations where it is illegal to own a Bible. In one Middle Eastern nation, a young boy read a story from a Christian magazine to his Muslim cousin, whose father then wanted to know more about the magazine and how he could get a copy of it. In restricted nations throughout the Middle East and Central Asia, believers must find creative ways to share the gospel and avoid drawing the attention of authorities.

Believers in Central Asia have endured oppression for decades, but there is movement toward greater openness for believers right now. Many Christian leaders are taking advantage of this opportunity to share the gospel as widely as possible while training Christian leaders of the next generation.

"I had nothing," said Dina, a former Muslim who came to Christ, "no money, just a bag of books. I started praying, and God gave me strength to persevere. I remembered a verse from the Bible: 'Take your cross and follow me.'"

Lord, thank You for the fruit of gospel seeds sown throughout the Middle East and Central Asia. Thank You for the inspiring example of our persecuted brothers and sisters as they suffer for righteousness' sake, boldly sharing the hope of Jesus Christ with their family, friends and persecutors. Please heal those whose faith has resulted in beatings and abuse, and cultivate joy in those who are committed to lives of suffering as Your witnesses. As our persecuted Christian family members experience Your faithfulness, may their obedience advance the gospel and bring glory to Your name. Amen.

SOUTH ASIA

God's kingdom continues to advance in South Asia through simple acts of obedience by Christ's witnesses. As a result, many are placing their trust in Christ and facing persecution by those opposed to the gospel. Family members, communities, Maoists, Islamists, Buddhists and Hindu nationalists all oppose the gospel in South Asia. But amid ongoing pressure from radical extremists and family members, our Christian brothers and sisters across South Asia persevere in faith and continue to proclaim the gospel of Jesus Christ.

In Nepal and India, the government has increasingly tried to stop the growth of God's kingdom, criminalizing Christian conversion and threatening to expel any person or organization engaged in preaching the gospel. The rise of radical Hinduism in India is empowered by those who hold to the *Hindutva* ideology of a "pure" Hindu nation. Christian converts are viewed as traitors to the Hindu homeland, and believers who boldly witness for Christ suffer beatings at the hands of Hindu nationalists as well as Maoists. Nevertheless, Christians in South Asia remain steadfast in faith and show radical forgiveness to their attackers as witnesses for Christ.

Christians in countries like Bangladesh and the Maldives endure opposition from Islamists and Muslim family members. And Islamic governments and radical Muslims close churches and imprison Christians under false charges in attempts to stop the advance of God's kingdom. When Muslims place their trust in Christ, they are often driven from their communities. But Muslim extremists are unsuccessful at preventing the spread of the gospel, as millions are turning to Christ through the bold and careful witness of His faithful followers.

Despite many obstacles, God's kingdom endures in South Asia through the faithful witness of our persecuted Christian family members. May their obedience inspire us toward a bold and faithful commitment to Christ at any cost.

Followers of Christ in India face opposition on multiple fronts. The vast majority of Indians are Hindus, while Muslims compose the second largest religious group. Still, Christians continue to gather for worship and proclaim the gospel boldly in this oppressive environment. After Hindu extremists murdered a pastor who had worked in India for more than two decades, his wife, Huldah, chose to continue ministering in the area rather than moving someplace safer.

"God has given me a vision for this area. I will not go anywhere else. The life is not easy, but I will still continue the work in this area because God has brought me here."

—Huldah

Hindus believe there are more than 330 million gods, yet radical Hindus in Nepal view Jesus Christ as a threat to their lives and culture. Pastor Chitria has been arrested multiple times for his ministry work in Nepal. The pastor, who considers the arrests an honor and privilege, helps prepare believers to remain faithful under persecution. He asks new Christians preparing for baptism seven questions, including whether they are willing to lose their family, friends and even their freedom to stand for Christ.

Bible distributors trek through Nepal's remote mountain regions to provide Bibles to those who cannot afford one or have no access to one. Distribution in these areas is challenging, but no trail is too difficult and no cost is too great to provide our persecuted Christian brothers and sisters with their own copies of God's Word.

As front-line workers trekked to remote Nepali villages to share the gospel, a local Hindu man accompanied them as a porter. He saw many people place their faith in Christ and heard the workers tell about a God who was loving and kind. As they continued their journey, the Christian workers shared God's truth with the Hindu man. And one day as the front-line workers were leading a woman to faith in Christ, they heard the Hindu man praying along with her. When they returned home after the journey, the man told them that he wanted to become a Christian. The front-line workers celebrated with him and his family as he publicly proclaimed his newfound faith.

As believers gathered for worship on Easter Sunday at Zion Church in Sri Lanka, they could not have imagined that an Islamist suicide bomber was about to detonate explosives in the church courtyard. Twelve-year-old Santhosh (*left*) suffered severe burns on his arms from the bombing. Although the attacker tried to silence their Christian witness, the members of Zion Church did not stop meeting after the bombing. They have continued to gather for worship every Sunday since the suicide attack.

After being driven from their home because of their Christian faith, a Nepali family said, "The Christian life is like a rose that blooms and spreads aroma in the midst of a thousand thorns." Believers in Nepal are persecuted by extremists among Hindu, Muslim, Buddhist and Marxist groups. Nevertheless, our Christian family members remain firm in their faith, bearing witness to Christ despite the risk.

Above: Hindu priests officiate *aarti*, a Hindu devotional ritual, on the Ganges River in Varanasi, India. Efforts by Hindu extremists to "purify" India by making it entirely Hindu have led to increased persecution of Christians throughout the country. Radical Hindus seek to appease Hindu deities by eliminating Christians, and they view Christian converts as traitors to the Hindu homeland. Even so, our brothers and sisters in India continue to study and obey God's Word at any cost.

A FATHER'S "CRIME"

RITESH

As a Hindu in India, Ritesh sought spiritual growth and enlightenment by reciting ritualistic prayers to Hindu gods. He had been longing for inner peace for decades when a local shopkeeper, Pascal, gave him a Bible. Reading the Bible daily, Ritesh found peace in the pages of God's Word, and he soon joined Pascal at church. After continuing to read the Bible and attend church and Bible study for several months, Ritesh abandoned Hinduism's lifeless idols for new life in Christ.

Ritesh and his family continued attending church, reading the Bible together for hours every morning, and sensing God's presence in their lives in a real and discernible way. And others noticed the change in their lives, too.

One day, men from a local Hindu temple warned Ritesh that if he and his family did not return to Hinduism, they would be reported to a Hindu nationalist organization. The group, in its efforts to establish a purely Hindu nation, is known to intimidate and beat new Christian converts.

A short time later, members of the nationalist group and other Hindu leaders gathered at Ritesh's house. They gave him and his family four days to abandon Christianity. And, as dozens of neighbors watched, one of the men forced Ritesh to surrender his Bible, journal and cellphone.

Within days, the mob returned, dragging Ritesh, his wife, Vanya, and their children to a Hindu temple to face 10 Hindu leaders. "Who do you worship," they demanded, "Jesus or the Hindu gods? Are you a Hindu or a Christian?"

Resolute, the family remained silent. "We will kill you if you don't leave Jesus," one leader threatened. Then, as Ritesh and Vanya's terrified children watched, the men began to beat the couple. And still they refused to speak.

The family was eventually released, but Ritesh was arrested for the "crime" of sharing the gospel with his family. As he sat in jail, the Hindu extremists continued to intimidate Vanya, ordering her to return to Hinduism.

"We will not go back," she told them.

After the authorities released Ritesh, he and his family relocated to a safer area. But he still sometimes sees their persecutors while driving his rickshaw. When he does, he simply shows them the love of Christ that has given him peace with God.

Lord, as Your kingdom advances in India, may Your truth supplant the false religions, ideologies and nationalism rooted in the hearts and minds of the people. Thank You, Father, for the forgiveness that persecuted Christians demonstrate toward those who oppose them. May the love they express win their persecutors to You, so that they too will seek to advance Your kingdom in every village. Amen.

NEPAL

BHUTAN

INDIA

BANGLADESH

SRI LANKA

MALDIVES

Commissioned in the 17th century by Shah Jahan as a tomb for his favorite wife, the Taj Mahal stands as a symbol of Muslim heritage in India. May it serve as a reminder to the global body of Christ to pray that God will open the eyes of Muslims, Buddhists, Hindus, Maoists and animists throughout South Asia to the truth found only in Jesus Christ.

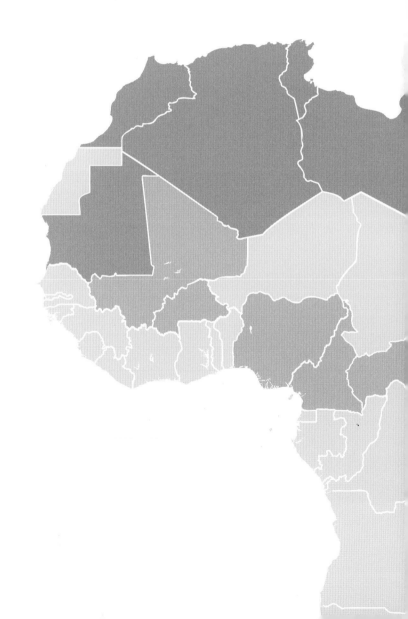

From remote villages in Nepal to crowded city streets in India, persecuted Christians proclaim the gospel across South Asia. Though many attempt to silence their witness, bold believers are willing to pay any price to witness for Christ. They walk in obedience to the Lord and are deeply encouraged when they learn that the global body of Christ is praying for them.

Let my prayer be counted as incense before you, and the lifting up of my hands as the evening sacrifice!

—Psalm 141:2

Above: A Christian front-line worker prays openly in front of a Hindu worship site on the Ganges River. The Ganges is considered sacred to Hindus, millions of whom wash in the river each year in the belief that it will cleanse them of their sins. Despite the intense persecution of Christian converts, hundreds of thousands of Hindus have come to Christ in this region in recent years. And God's kingdom continues to advance even as opposition to the Christian faith and witness grows in many parts of India.

"Even if they destroy our building, we will still worship together under a tree. We cannot stop worshiping. When persecution comes, our faith becomes more and more strong."

—Rashir, from Bangladesh, after radical Buddhists attacked his church

Facing page: Surjah, Kolah and Krishna rejected animism after experiencing the power of Christ in their lives. But when the wife of a church member died, villagers accused the three men of murder because they had prayed for her. After spending more than nine months in prison, where they led 13 other prisoners to faith in Christ, the men emerged even more committed to sharing the gospel.

Above: A woman smiles joyfully after receiving her new Bible on a sunny morning in Nepal. While Bibles are legal there, Bible distribution is opposed by extremist groups. The small Christian population is under increasing pressure to reject Jesus Christ as the country's leaders attempt to create a Hindu nation. The Bible is crucial to believers' faith and perseverance, as many are harassed or beaten for following Christ.

Above and upper right: Fedu and Shukkur are reaching people with the gospel in Bangladesh. A former Muslim, Fedu is determined to tell other Muslims about the hope he's found in Christ. "I am going out and sharing my faith," he said. He has led an imam to Christ and asks for prayer as he shares the gospel with many others.

Above: Churches can gather and worship openly in Sri Lanka, but they are pressured by the government to register, and local governments sometimes attack pastors and churches. Despite such hostility, Sri Lankan Christians continue to plant churches and send missionaries to advance God's kingdom throughout the world.

> The light shines in the darkness, and the darkness has not overcome it.
>
> —John 1:5

Christians in India preach the gospel boldly among radical Hindus and militant Muslims. Hani, a former Hindu, and Chakama, a former Muslim, have actively shared their faith ever since coming to know Christ and getting married. When they were kicked out of their village because of their bold witness, they moved to another city and planted a church that grew to more than 55 families. Hani and Chakama also started two prayer meetings in surrounding villages. Although Chakama's family continues to threaten her for leaving Islam, she remains faithful to Christ. And though their community opposes the church, they continue to gather for worship, and the church continues to grow.

THE "CURSED" WIDOW

TAVESA

Once a month, Tavesa invites six women to her small, dilapidated home in Nepal. The women read Scripture and pray, ignoring the idols and pictures of Hindu gods peering blindly at them from nearby tables and surrounding walls.

When Tavesa's husband died eight years ago, her 24-year-old son took over her home and forced her to move into his run-down house. As a zealous Hindu, he insisted that she leave the idols and pictures of his favorite gods where he had placed them.

Tavesa became a Christian two years after her husband died, when she received healing through the prayers of a Christian in her village. Leaving Hinduism and placing her faith in Christ did nothing to improve her earthly status, but as a widow she was already considered cursed.

In Nepal's predominantly Hindu culture, a widow has no status. For at least the first year following her husband's death, a widow must wear white. And she is often blamed for her husband's death, regardless of the actual cause. Many who see one of Nepal's roughly 500,000 widows avoid them in public, believing the widow's bad luck could be transferred to them.

Tavesa's son believes he is honoring his father by ensuring that his family remains Hindu. And Tavesa can't challenge him because he is now the head of the family.

The boldest act she has taken — other than publicly professing faith in Christ — was hanging a cross on her wall. But one of her daughters took it down, believing it would anger the Hindu gods.

Tavesa's grown children aren't the only ones opposed to her Christian faith. Of the approximately 200 families in her village, only two are Christian. And her neighbors often pressure her to stop attending church and to return to Hinduism.

Still, Tavesa's faith remains firm through her continual study of God's Word. Having read and deeply considered Matthew 5:44, in which Jesus tells us to love our enemies and pray for those who persecute us, she said, "I am praying for them because they are not persecuting me, but they are persecuting Jesus."

Tavesa prays that her adult son and daughters will come to know Christ, and she has seen hopeful signs that her son's heart is starting to soften. Although Tavesa lives alone, she said she knows God is with her.

"I am alone nowhere," she said. "Jesus is with me, and there are so many people praying for me. So I am not alone."

Right: Hindus in India celebrate the Holi festival, known as the festival of colors, to signal the beginning of spring. For them, it is symbolic of the triumph of good over evil. As participants throw colored powder into the air and on each other, they exalt Hindu deities in a colorful display of devotion and celebration. Pray that those lost in the darkness of Hinduism throughout South Asia will come to know Christ, who triumphs over all and gives victory over sin and death (1 Cor. 15:57).

Jesus said, "Let the little children come to me and do not hinder them, for to such belongs the kingdom of heaven."

—Matthew 19:14

Right: For many in South Asia, owning a Bible comes with the risk of hostility and violence. In Nepal, a woman who came to faith in Christ was beaten by her Hindu husband with her own Bible. VOM replaced her Bible, and she is gaining literacy by reading the Bible every day with her son. In India, a Christian woman's husband tore her Bible to pieces after discovering that she had left Hinduism to follow Christ. VOM replaced her Bible as well, and her husband's heart has softened toward her Christian faith as he has observed her reading and studying God's Word. "My Bible is everything to me," she said. "It is the living Word of God. Without it, I can't live."

Right: A man participates in a Hindu ceremonial parade in Sri Lanka. Northern Sri Lanka is mostly Hindu, while the southern part of the country is majority Buddhist. Christians are persecuted in both areas, but that does not stop them from sharing the gospel. One pastor, who has ministered in the country for decades, has had his home burglarized and burned multiple times by Buddhist monks who oppose his ministry. Despite this opposition, he has planted several churches in the area and meets regularly with the police chief for Bible study and discipleship.

"Many came from far around the world ... and we were strengthened by God. We were able to see the love of God through the people who generously came."

—Sri Lankan pastor, on support from the body of Christ after his church was bombed

Our brothers and sisters in Christ share the gospel in Bangladesh knowing that they risk opposition from local authorities, Islamic extremists and even their own family members. Shemul, a former Muslim, passionately tells others in his village about the hope he has found in Christ. Despite threats from family members and neighbors, he continues to bear witness to the truth of Christ. "This Jesus who saved my soul can save my body also," he said. "Jesus taught me to share what I believe with others. I cannot stop, so I must go and teach. I received the gift, so I want my people to get the same gift of salvation."

Facing page: These seven Christian men were wrongly charged with the murder that ignited the Kandhamal riots in India in 2008. They spent 11 years in prison before their eventual release. During their imprisonment, they were encouraged by God's Word and the prayers of other believers. And despite all they went through, they continue to follow Christ with bold faith. "Every Sunday, I go and I share the gospel," one of them said.

Thank You, heavenly Father, for the faith of our brothers and sisters in South Asia. Please heal those who are suffering for Your name, and provide for those who lack the daily necessities of life. Thank You for their example of love as they pray for and share the Good News with those who hate them and want to silence their witness. Embolden our persecuted Christian family members to continue advancing the gospel in the face of opposition. And may their testimonies of perseverance and joy inspire boldness for Your name's sake throughout the global body of Christ! Amen.

ASIA PACIFIC

After enduring decades of oppression and persecution by Communist governments and extremist groups, Christians in parts of the Asia Pacific region have grown accustomed to worshiping in underground settings and sharing the gospel through creative means. While our persecuted Christian brothers and sisters face significant opposition in many parts of the region, they continue to boldly follow Christ despite the risk.

Under North Korea's Communist-inspired dictatorship, Christianity is considered subversive. Anyone who even expresses interest in Christianity is labeled an enemy of the state, and believers are sent to prisons and labor camps, where many die from starvation, overwork and torture. The government expects citizens to report those, including friends and family members, who show a lack of devotion to the regime. But despite social pressure and the threat of persecution, Christians in North Korea hold firmly to their faith, creatively smuggling Bibles into the country and carefully sharing the gospel.

In China, millions of Christians must worship in illegal house churches, as only government-controlled churches can operate legally. Amid unrelenting pressure and oppression from the Communist government, Chinese house-church leaders refuse to compromise the gospel, working to advance God's kingdom in the face of increasingly restrictive religious regulations.

In places like Laos and Vietnam, the government restricts some Christian activities. Believers there face opposition mainly from local authorities and community members who target them in rural and tribal regions. These Christians often lose their jobs and are driven from their homes and villages for following Christ, yet churches continue to grow through their bold witness.

In other parts of the Asia Pacific region, Christians face hostility from Buddhists and Muslims as well as family members who reject them for leaving their traditional religions for Christ. In Myanmar, churches continue to grow despite persecution by the government and the Buddhist majority, while in Malaysia, the government strictly opposes outreach and evangelism among the Malay people. Malay culture is closely identified with Islam, but many indigenous people have come to know Christ in one part of the country. In Indonesia, where Islamic extremists seek to silence the gospel, bold evangelists are leading Muslims to Christ by actively sharing their faith amid persecution from local governments and community members.

In some of the most restricted nations in the world, our Christian family members in the Asia Pacific region resolve to live in obedience to Christ and bear witness to the hope of the gospel at any cost.

Right: A young girl in Myanmar receives a backpack filled with basic necessities and a Bible during a Christmas Care distribution. Front-line workers distribute backpacks like this one to children of persecuted Christians in restricted nations and hostile areas. The contents are tailored to the needs of the children in each region, and every pack comes with a full-color, illustrated children's Bible in the appropriate language. For most of these children, it is the first Bible they have ever received.

Some Buddhist families in countries like Myanmar send their children to monasteries for training at a very young age, and the children of Muslim families in Indonesia attend primary schools where they focus on memorizing the Quran. These children spend hours each day memorizing Buddhist or Muslim texts under threat of abuse and with little rest. Grounding children in the truth of God's Word is essential to advancing God's kingdom in regions like these, where many seek to silence their Christian witness.

And how are they to preach unless they are sent? As it is written, "How beautiful are the feet of those who preach the good news!"

—Romans 10:15

Whether by land, air or water, front-line workers deliver Bibles to some of the most remote areas in restricted nations and hostile areas. Equipping believers with God's Word comes with the daily risk of being caught and persecuted by Communist authorities or other enemies of the gospel. Despite the risk, our faithful Christian brothers and sisters work tirelessly to distribute Bibles to those who have little access to it.

TEACHING THE ILLEGAL GOSPEL

BOUPHA

As 18-year-old Boupha led a group of children in a Bible story one Sunday morning, her Sunday school class was interrupted by the police. "The kids were shocked and afraid," Boupha recalls. "I was also afraid because this had never happened before."

When Boupha was 15, she began attending church with a friend. As she observed Christians singing songs of praise, reading the Bible, and worshiping joyfully, she yearned to know the God they followed. And after placing her faith in Christ, she immediately looked for ways to serve at church.

"I wanted to serve the Lord in some way," she said. "I wanted to see the spiritual growth of the kids in my church to follow God's way."

Boupha soon began teaching Sunday school. And about a year later, she received a visit from the police. "Did you know that teaching these little kids here is against the law?" the officers asked threateningly.

Scared and shaken, Boupha started praying. "Lord, please help me. Give me wisdom in this situation. Give me wisdom in answering whatever questions they have."

When the officers asked her who was paying her to teach, Boupha truthfully insisted that she was teaching voluntarily. And when they questioned her about her Christian beliefs, she courageously shared the gospel with them.

The policemen asked no further questions but confiscated Boupha's teaching materials. Seeing an opportunity, she encouraged the officers to study the materials themselves, hoping what they learned might lead them to faith in Christ.

Boupha left the interrogation with a greater resolve to continue teaching children about Christ, and she continues to serve in her church, helping lead worship as well as youth Bible studies. Although she is judged and ridiculed by peers, she is unashamed of following Christ.

"To be [humiliated] for Jesus is a good thing," she says. "I am willing and open to accept persecution if it comes again. It has taught me to keep my faith in the Lord and that He is always with me. Jesus did everything for me. I will not back away from the Lord."

"Now I am tired physically, but my heart is not tired for the Lord's work."

—Bounsaen, a 101-year-old Christian in Laos

Before becoming a Christian, Chau was a heavy drinker and didn't work. But after coming to know Christ, she became a new person. When her daughter was expecting a baby, Chau left her Vietnamese village to stay with her daughter for a few weeks. While she was away, her neighbors sent word that she was not welcome back in the village because she was a Christian. And when Chau tried to return home, the villagers stopped her and told her they were confiscating several acres of prime farming land that Chau had inherited from her grandparents.

Ethnic minority groups like the Hmong and Khmu are found throughout Vietnam, Laos and China. Many of them follow animistic tribal beliefs, but front-line workers have planted house churches among the Khmu, who have increasingly turned to faith in Christ. And as these churches have grown, so has persecution. Village authorities confiscate Christians' land and refuse to allow them to farm. Nevertheless, God's kingdom continues to advance among these ethnic groups.

Despite intense opposition, God's kingdom is advancing in Laos through the bold faith of young Christians. Peng, 14, shared about Christ many times with her friend, Sa. Sa eventually came to faith in Christ even though village leaders have persecuted Christians in the past and some villagers hate Christians. When Sa's parents learned that she had trusted Christ and was attending church, they yelled at her for following "the religion of foreigners." Sa remained firm in her faith, and her parents kicked her out of their home because of her decision to follow Christ.

North Korea is one of the most restricted nations on earth, and its border is among the most tightly controlled. Christian worship is brutally opposed and is considered subversive to the oppressive regime founded by Kim Il Sung. But despite restrictive laws, economic hardship, imprisonment and even death, our brothers and sisters hold fast to their faith, some daring to smuggle God's Word into the country.

Heavenly Father, may Your redemptive purposes be accomplished throughout the Asia Pacific region, no matter the opposition. May our persecuted brothers and sisters model Christ's forgiveness and be ambassadors of grace to those who try to silence them. As light dispels darkness, please cause the light of Your truth to dispel evil and keep our persecuted Christian family members safe from those who would wish them harm. May Your kingdom advance and Your name be glorified in and through our Christian brothers and sisters in the Asia Pacific region. Amen.

NORTH KOREA

PHILIPPINES
(MINDANAO)

From the foothills of China to the guarded borders of North Korea to the coastlines of Indonesia, our brothers and sisters throughout the Asia Pacific region follow Christ with a bold and unwavering faith. Amid threats and oppression from Communists, Buddhists and Muslims, believers continue to share the gospel, gather for worship and make disciples in obedience to Christ and His Great Commission, no matter the cost.

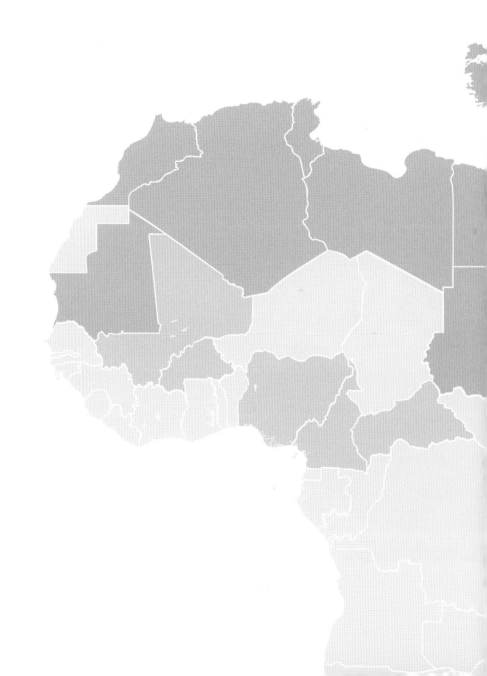

Islamic extremists take every effort to silence the Christian witness of our Indonesian brothers and sisters. Suicide bombers have attacked churches, and radical Muslims harass even those worshiping in their own homes. While one Christian family was in the middle of family worship, a Muslim neighbor burst into their house and told them they could not hold a Christian meeting in their home. The neighbor waved a stick at the Christians and warned them that he would return with a mob if they did not stop their worship.

After World War II, the Korean Peninsula was divided into two zones, known as South Korea and North Korea. Prior to Korea's division, the north was a thriving center of Christian worship. Pyongyang, the capital, was known as "the Jerusalem of the East" in the early 1900s because of its more than 2,000 churches. But decades of government oppression forced Christians underground. And now in North Korea, anyone discovered to be a Christian or to express interest in Christ or the Bible is considered an enemy of the state.

"How wonderful it would be if, because of this suffering, we might be able to give off the sweet fragrance of the gospel!"

—Li Yingqiang, Early Rain Church, China

The gospel of Christ continues to spread throughout China despite opposition from the country's Communist government. Though hundreds of church leaders have been detained and arrested, our Chinese brothers and sisters boldly obey Christ's imperative that we gather for worship and make disciples. Their commitment to sharing the Good News is a burning and shining lamp amid China's efforts to eradicate any witness for Christ.

INSIDE A CHINESE PRISON

LEO

When the police summoned Leo for questioning, he expected to be arrested. The day before, a local printing company had called to tell him that police had seized factory records and knew that he had commissioned the printing of several thousand unofficial Bibles (unregistered with the Chinese government). With limited options, Leo reported to the police, who took him to a detention center after hours of interrogation.

Upon arriving at his cell, Leo was shocked to see 50 to 60 people crammed into a space of about 500 square feet. Despite his fear, Leo adjusted to life in the detention center. And within a few days, he received a visit from his attorney, who told him to expect the worst. Leo learned that it could be a month before he was even officially arrested.

Then came the waiting. Leo watched as other prisoners came and went from the cell, while he heard no news of his own case. After 34 days, authorities finally issued the arrest warrant, and Leo knew he was in for a long ordeal.

Conditions in the jail were worse than Leo could have imagined. The food was hard to swallow, and prisoners slept on boards on a concrete floor with blankets so filthy that he had to plug his nose just to sleep. At night, after everyone else was asleep, Leo would pray, "Oh, Lord, all that I have done was for You. Why have You allowed me to face persecution? Is It because my faith is small that You test me? Or is it because You are preparing me for a new mission?"

Leo eventually was indicted on charges that carried a penalty of up to three years in prison. In the end, he was released after a year in prison, a period he later described as "physical, mental and spiritual training." Although life in the detention center was hard and Leo spent many days wondering about his future, he still had peace. "I knew that God, whom I depended on, would save me," he said. "When I recall [my time in prison], I think of it as life training. God will not let this training be in vain. God will show me His will for the future, and this experience will be my source of faith and my motivation to move forward."

"The main point is that we forgive the people who did what happened. We pray for others like them, that God can give them grace to repent. The Great Commission is our task. We must share the gospel."

—Pastor Yonathan, an Indonesian pastor whose church was bombed

Above and right: Indonesia has the largest Muslim population in the world, and Islamist violence has led many Muslims there to question Islam and be more open to the gospel. While Christians can worship openly in Indonesia, it is illegal to share the gospel. Nevertheless, bold evangelists continue to tell Muslims about the love of Christ and lead them to faith in Him. Pray that new Christians will be grounded in God's Word.

People in rural China have the least access to the gospel. Copies of God's Word are difficult to find and too expensive for many to purchase even when they are available. VOM works to deliver Bibles to all in these areas who need a copy of God's Word.

Above: Khin persecuted Christians for decades as a Buddhist in Myanmar, until he had a life-changing encounter with six pastors while in prison. Since coming to faith in Christ, he has served the Lord by sharing the gospel in villages throughout Myanmar.

> "Look, I tell you, lift up your eyes, and see that the fields are white for harvest."
>
> —John 4:35b

Front-line workers share the gospel with members of the Hmong ethnic group in Vietnam, Laos, Thailand and Myanmar, and those who follow Christ often pay a price. In one Laotian village, authorities refused to distribute rice to Hmong Christians during a drought, saying the Hmong must renounce their Christian faith if they want help. But despite harsh persecution, the Hmong are turning to Christ in growing numbers.

"For me to accept Christ and be persecuted, the Scriptures are fulfilled. For this I am grateful to the Lord. The Bible teaches us to forgive 70 times seven. I definitely have to forgive, but sometimes it is difficult."

—Paing, a former Buddhist monk in Myanmar who was persecuted for sharing the gospel in Buddhist villages

More than three-quarters of the people in Myanmar are Buddhists, and Buddhist monks there actively oppose Christian converts and evangelists. A front-line worker who has been threatened and beaten for his Christian witness continues to advance God's kingdom in Myanmar, asking the global body of Christ to pray for the salvation of his countrymen. "Please pray that the Burmese people will come to know Jesus," he said.

Right: Front-line workers travel for hours by motorcycle over muddy roads and traffic-filled streets to deliver Bibles in Southeast Asia. After learning that a front-line worker had sold his motorcycle to fund church-planting efforts, VOM provided the worker with a new motorcycle. He now visits villages hundreds of miles away from his home to share the Good News. "I enjoy riding the motorcycle because whenever I want to stop to share the gospel, I can do that," he said.

Our brothers and sisters in Myanmar face severe persecution from those who oppose their Christian faith. In one village, a man was fined and shackled for three days for buying a banana from a Christian vendor in the market. After his release, he sought out a pastor, who led the man and two of his friends to faith in Christ. The man then led several other villagers to faith in Christ and invited the pastor to lead a worship service in the village. Angry Buddhist villagers then interrupted the service, severely beating the pastor and throwing stones at the worshipers. But the Christians remained firm in their faith. "As much as I can, I'm sharing the Good News and I will continue to do so," the man said.

"Before I was a Christian, I was so poor. I was half-dead, hopeless and not knowing anything. Once I accepted Christ, I was full of joy — so much joy that I wanted to share this."

—Sun, a Christian woman who was kicked out of her village in Laos for sharing the gospel

In some parts of Myanmar, people live in floating villages. And clandestine churches sometimes meet in stilt houses raised above the water.

And Jesus said to them, "Follow me, and I will make you become fishers of men."

—Mark 1:17

Dear heavenly Father, may every people hear Your gospel in the Asia Pacific region. Please continue to strengthen, encourage and embolden persecuted believers to continue sharing the Good News with their neighbors.

As our persecuted Christian family members work to advance God's kingdom throughout the Asia Pacific region, may their testimonies of faithfulness and obedience inspire us to a closer walk with Christ. May we also boldly proclaim the gospel in our families and neighborhoods, with an unwavering commitment to following Christ at any cost.

THE JOURNEY OF
FELLOWSHIP CONTINUES

Thank you for joining this visual journey to some of the world's most difficult and dangerous mission fields, where our persecuted brothers and sisters in Christ advance God's kingdom at great cost.

Richard and Sabina Wurmbrand, founders of The Voice of the Martyrs, began their journey of faith in 1938 when they placed their trust in Christ in their homeland of Romania. As they reached out to Nazis and, later, Russian Communists with the gospel, they paid dearly, suffering arrests, interrogations and imprisonment. Richard spent a total of 14 years in prison for his faithful witness, and Sabina spent three years in prison.

Amid their imprisonment and oppression under an atheistic Communist regime, Richard and Sabina experienced fellowship with members of the global body of Christ who prayed for them and risked much to bring them help. Richard wrote,

> *During the years I was imprisoned, God had moved wonderfully. The Underground Church was no longer abandoned and forgotten. Americans and other Christians had begun to help us and pray for us.*
>
> *My family and I would not have survived without the material help I received from praying Christians abroad. The same is true with many other underground pastors and martyrs in Communist countries. I can testify out of my own experience about the material and even greater moral help that has been given to us by special missions formed for this purpose in the free world. For us, these believers were like angels sent by God!*

Your prayers and gifts continue to strengthen and encourage persecuted Christians today. When they receive help from the global body of Christ, they know they are neither alone nor forgotten.

We pray that the photographs and text in this book will continue to help you envision the lives of our persecuted brothers and sisters in Christ on the frontlines as you lift them up before our heavenly Father. May this journey of fellowship inspire you to a deeper commitment to Christ and His Great Commission — at any cost!

ABOUT THE VOICE OF THE MARTYRS

The Voice of the Martyrs (VOM) is a nonprofit, interdenominational Christian organization dedicated to serving persecuted Christians on the world's most difficult and dangerous mission fields and bringing other members of the body of Christ into fellowship with them. VOM was founded in 1967 by Pastor Richard Wurmbrand and his wife, Sabina. Richard was imprisoned 14 years in Communist Romania for his faith in Christ, and Sabina was imprisoned for three years. They were ransomed out of Romania in 1965 and soon established a global network of missions dedicated to assisting persecuted Christians.

To be inspired by the courageous faith of our persecuted brothers and sisters in Christ who are advancing the gospel in hostile areas and restricted nations, request a free subscription to VOM's award-winning monthly magazine. Visit us at vom.org, or call 800-747-0085.

To learn more about VOM offices around the world, visit vom.org/about.

DIRK WILLEMS
1569
TURNED BACK TO SAVE THE BOUNTY HUNTER CHASING HIM WHO HAD FALLEN THROUGH THE ICE; BURNED AT THE STAKE AFTER HIS ARREST.

MOHAMMED SAEED
2002
HIS THROAT WAS SLIT BY A RELATIVE AFTER HE REFUSED TO RENOUNCE CHRIST AND RETURN TO ISLAM.

MATTHEW
60
BEHEADED IN ETHIOPIA.

MATTHIAS
70
STONED TO DEATH IN JERUSALEM.

NICHOLAS RIDLEY AND HUGH LATIMER
1555
BURNED AT THE STAKE. "WE SHALL THIS DAY LIGHT SUCH A CANDLE BY GOD'S GRACE, IN ENGLAND, AS I TRUST NEVER SHALL BE PUT OUT."

MINKA HANSKAMP AND MARGARET MORGAN
1974
WHEN GUERRILLAS IN THAILAND TOLD THE TWO MISSIONARY NURSES THEY WERE TO BE KILLED, THEY SAID, "GIVE US A LITTLE TIME TO READ AND PRAY."

JOHN PATON
1684
"FAREWELL ALL WORLDLY ENJOYMENTS. AND WELCOME, FATHER, SON AND HOLY SPIRIT."

MULLAH ASSAD ULLAH
2004
THE TALIBAN WAS ANGRY WHEN THIS FORMER MUSLIM LEADER BECAME A FOLLOWER OF CHRIST; HIS THROAT WAS SLIT AT THE MARKET AND HIS BODY DRAGGED THROUGH IT AS A WARNING TO OTHER MUSLIMS NOT TO ACCEPT CHRIST.

CATHERINE SAUBE
1417
BURNED AT THE STAKE.

JOHN AND BETTY STAM
1934
KILLED BY COMMUNISTS IN CHINA. "AS FOR US MAY GOD BE GLORIFIED, WHETHER BY LIFE OR BY DEATH."

IMMANUEL ANDEGERESGH AND KIBROM FIREMICHEL
2006
TORTURED TO DEATH AFTER BEING ARRESTED AT A SECRET CHURCH MEETING IN ERITREA.

SERGEI BESSARAB
2004
SHOT AND KILLED AFTER PLANTING A CHURCH IN A TAJIK CITY WHERE THERE WERE 146 MOSQUES, BUT NO CHRISTIAN PRESENCE.

JAMES GORDON
1872
KILLED BY A BLOW FROM A STONE AXE AS HE SAT TRANSLATING STEPHEN'S WORDS IN ACTS 7:60. "LORD, DO NOT CHARGE THEM WITH THIS SIN."

HENRY VOES, JOHANN ECK AND LAMPERTUS THORN
1523
"WE BELIEVE GOD'S COMMANDMENTS, AND NOT HUMAN STATUTES, SAVE OR CONDEMN."

REVEREND WAU
2003
STRANGLED IN INDONESIA AFTER HE CONTINUED CHURCH MEETINGS IN SPITE OF MUSLIM THREATS.

JANANI LUWUM
1977
ACCUSED OF TREASON BY IDI AMIN AND EXECUTED IN UGANDA.

THERESIA, ALFITA AND YARNI
2005
ON THE WAY TO THEIR CHRISTIAN SCHOOL, THESE THREE CHRISTIAN GIRLS WERE BEHEADED BY RADICAL MUSLIM JIHAD WARRIORS.

JOHN BROWN
1685
"I HAVE NO MORE TO DO BUT DIE."

JOHN NESBIT
1685
"MY SOUL DOTH LONG TO BE FREED OF BODILY INFIRMITIES AND EARTHLY ORGANS, THAT SO I MAY FLEE TO HIS ROYAL PALACE."

JOSEPH MUCOSA BALIKUDDEMBE
1885
CONDEMNED TO BE BURNED, HE REFUSED TO BE BOUND. "WHY BIND ME? DO YOU THINK I SHALL FLEE? FLEE WHERE, TO GOD?"

BALTHASAR HUBMAIER
1528
BURNED AT THE STAKE ON MARCH 10, 1528, AS HIS WIFE ELIZABETH URGED HIM TO BE STRONG. THREE DAYS AFTER HIS EXECUTION, ELIZABETH WAS THROWN INTO THE DANUBE RIVER WITH A ROCK AROUND HER NECK.

VALENTINUS
CA. 269
BEATEN BY CLUBS AND BEHEADED ON FEBRUARY 14.

YESU DASU
2000
KILLED IN INDIA FOR PREACHING THE GOSPEL TO THE "UNTOUCHABLES," THE LOWEST CASTE HINDUS.

JOHN HOOPER
1555
BURNED AT THE STAKE; "DEATH IS NO DEATH, BUT MEANS TO LIVE."

AROUN VORAPHORN
2005
FAITHFUL PREACHER, MURDERED IN LAOS.

JAMES ABDULKARIM YAHAYA
2001
KILLED IN HIS APARTMENT IN ABUJA, NIGERIA, AFTER LEAVING ISLAM TO FOLLOW CHRIST.

EUSEBIO FERRAO
2006
HIS BODY—BEATEN, STABBED, STRANGLED AND SMOTHERED— WAS LEFT IN A POOL OF HIS OWN BLOOD AT THE FRONT OF HIS CHURCH IN INDIA.

WANG ZHIMING
1973
KILLED BY COMMUNISTS; HIS LAST WORDS ENCOURAGED OTHERS TO FOLLOW CHRIST.

JAMES RENWICK
1688
"I GO TO YOUR GOD AND MY GOD. DEATH TO ME IS A BED TO THE WEARY."

HUGH MCKAIL
1666
AS HE STOOD ON THE GALLOWS, SAID, "AND NOW I BEGIN MY INTERCOURSE WITH GOD, WHICH SHALL NEVER BE BROKEN OFF."

SAMUEL MASIH
2004
KILLED IN THE HOSPITAL BY A PAKISTANI POLICEMAN, WHO SAID, "I WANTED TO EARN A PLACE IN PARADISE BY KILLING HIM."

JOHN PENRY
1593
HANGED, HIS LAST WORDS TO HIS FOUR DAUGHTERS BEGAN "I, YOUR FATHER, NOW READY TO GIVE MY LIFE," AND CHARGED THEM TO BRING UP THEIR CHILDREN TO FOLLOW CHRIST FAITHFULLY.

GRAHAM STAINES
1999
BURNED TO DEATH IN HIS CAR, ALONG WITH HIS TWO YOUNG SONS, BY RADICAL HINDUS IN INDIA.

JAMES HANNINGTON
1885
"IF THIS IS THE LAST CHAPTER OF EARTHLY HISTORY, THEN THE NEXT WILL BE THE FIRST PAGE OF THE HEAVENLY—NO BLOTS OR SMUDGES, NO INCOHERENCE, BUT SWEET CONVERSE IN THE PRESENCE OF THE LAMB."

MARGARET WILSON AND MARGARET MACLACHLAN
1685
TIED TO STAKES AT LOW TIDE AND THEN DROWNED AS THE TIDE CAME IN.

JAMES GUTHRIE
1661
"I WOULD NOT EXCHANGE THIS SCAFFOLD WITH THE PALACE AND MITRE OF THE GREATEST PRELATE IN BRITAIN."

MARTIN RAY BURNHAM
2002
MISSIONARY TO THE PHILIPPINES; HE WAS TAKEN HOSTAGE AND EVENTUALLY KILLED BY A MUSLIM TERRORIST GROUP.

PASTOR IRIANTO KONGKOLI
2006
SHOT IN THE BACK OF THE HEAD AT POINT-BLANK RANGE IN INDONESIA.

ALLEN GARDINER
1851
"LORD, AT YOUR FEET I HUMBLY FALL. AND I GIVE YOU ALL I HAVE. ALL THAT YOUR LOVE REQUIRES. TAKE CARE OF ME IN THIS HOUR OF TEST. DO NOT LET ME HAVE THE THOUGHTS OF A COMPLAINER. MAKE ME FEEL YOUR POWER, WHICH GIVES ME LIFE."

JOHN KENSIT
1902
HIT BY A HURLED METAL FILE AFTER A SERVICE WHERE HE HAD PREACHED.

SUSIANTY TINULELE
2004
GUNNED DOWN ONE SUNDAY EVENING IN THE PULPIT OF HER CHURCH IN SULAWESI, INDONESIA.

JIANG ZONGXIU
2004
TORTURED TO DEATH BY CHINESE POLICE AFTER BEING ARRESTED FOR HANDING OUT CHRISTIAN LITERATURE IN THE VILLAGE MARKET.

DULAL SARKAR
2005
KILLED BY RADICAL MUSLIMS. WHEN THEY TOLD HIM TO STOP MINISTRY, HE REPLIED, "I WILL NOT STOP THE MINISTRY GOD HAS CALLED ME TO PERFORM."

SIMON THE ZEALOT
74
MISSIONARY TO NORTH AFRICA AND WESTERN EUROPE; SAWN IN HALF.

PREM KUMAR
2006
AN INVITATION TO LEAD A PRAYER SERVICE WAS A RUSE TO GET KUMAR; HIS BODY WAS FOUND THE NEXT MORNING.

MARY DYER
1660
HUNG IN MASSACHUSETTS. "I CAME IN OBEDIENCE TO THE WILL OF GOD."

TAPON ROY AND LIPLAL MARANDI
2005
THOUGH ORDERED TO STOP SHOWING THE JESUS FILM IN BANGLADESH, THEY FELT CALLED TO CONTINUE. RADICAL MUSLIMS STABBED THEM BOTH TO DEATH.

ESTHER JOHN
1960
KILLED IN PAKISTAN AFTER REFUSING HER PARENTS' INSTRUCTIONS TO MARRY A MUSLIM MAN.

JOHN OLDCASTLE
1417
HE WAS HOISTED BY CHAINS BETWEEN TWO GALLOWS AND A LOW FIRE SET BENEATH HIM. THROUGHOUT HIS AGONY, HE IS SAID TO HAVE PRAISED GOD AND COMMENDED HIS SOUL TO GOD'S KEEPING.

SUNDAY NACHE ACHI
2004
RADICAL MUSLIMS CAME TO HIS DORM ROOM AND SNATCHED THE UNIVERSITY STUDENT; HIS BODY WAS FOUND THE NEXT DAY.

JOHN WILLIAMS
1839
ATTACKED AND KILLED AT ERROMANGO, NEW HEBRIDES, HIS BODY WAS EATEN BY THE ISLANDERS.

THE NAGASAKI MARTYRS
1597
TWENTY-SIX MEN WERE CRUCIFIED ON NISHIZAKA HILL ON CROSSES CUT TO FIT THE DIMENSIONS OF EACH OF THE CONDEMNED. WHEN THE COLUMN OF PRISONERS SAW THEIR CROSSES LYING IN THE WHEAT FIELD BESIDE THE HILL, THEY EACH EMBRACED THEIR CROSS.

ROBERT THOMAS
1865
FIRST PROTESTANT MISSIONARY TO KOREA; AFTER HE GOT OFF THE SHIP HE OFFERED A BIBLE TO A SOLDIER WHO THEN KILLED HIM ON THE RIVERBANK.

BITRUS MANJANG
2002
CHURCH LEADER IN NIGERIA KILLED IN A MUSLIM ATTACK.

LADY JANE GREY
1554
"FATHER, INTO YOUR HANDS I COMMIT MY SPIRIT."

JUDE/THADDAEUS
CA. 70
EXECUTED WITH ARROWS IN PRESENT-DAY ARMENIA.

AHMAD EL-ACHWAL
2004
SHOT TO DEATH IN LEBANON AFTER HE REJECTED WARNINGS TO LEAVE CHRISTIANITY AND RETURN TO ISLAM.